# JOHN CHARLES RYLE

## 1816–1900

# JOHN CHARLES RYLE

## 1816–1900

### Marcus L. Loane

**HODDER AND STOUGHTON**
LONDON SYDNEY AUCKLAND TORONTO

**British Library Cataloguing in Publication Data**

Loane, Marcus L.
  John Charles Ryle, 1816–1900.—(Hodder Christian paperbacks)
  1. Ryle, John Charles    2. Church of England—Biography
  I. Title
  283'.092'4    BX5199.R/

ISBN 0 340 34251 X

*Hodder and Stoughton Editorial Office: 47 Bedford Square, London WC1B 3DP*

To

The Right Reverend

Timothy Dudley-Smith

Bishop of Thetford

Commissary for the Archbishop of Sydney

In token of appreciation

for counsel and friendship

# CONTENTS

# FOREWORD

by

## THE RIGHT REV. TIMOTHY DUDLEY-SMITH

This is a book that has been maturing over the years. Sir Marcus Loane published a short biography of Ryle in 1953, when he was Vice-Principal of Moore Theological College. In 1967 a rather more detailed study appeared in *Makers of our Heritage*, written when he was Archbishop of Sydney. Now, as the first-fruits of his retirement from the Primacy, and in the light of historical information which has become available more recently, we have this present book. It has been well worth waiting for.

Why is Bishop Ryle of such importance as to demand three studies from the same pen? Not solely for his pastoral ministry, or his twenty years' episcopate as first bishop of Liverpool; not even as "the Prince of tract writers" whose books and pamphlets sold by the million, and sell today. Surely, rather, for what the Islington Clerical Meeting, in their farewell address on his retirement, called "his witness for Scriptural truth, a witness equally strong and wise".

Ryle marked out a path for Evangelical churchmen in days when much of the Church of England was drifting on the tides of liberalism or tractarianism. In a direct and simple style, carefully cultivated to reach the man in the pew and the man in the street, he deployed historical acumen, theological study, and, above all, biblical exposition to set forth the timeless truth of the Gospel, and to uphold the formularies of his Church as true to the New Testament. He did this firmly, courageously and earnestly throughout his ministry, not primarily as a controversialist, but as a pastor and evangelist. It is a task that needs doing in every generation, not least in our own. In this study, through the events of Ryle's life, through his own writings, and his auto-biographical memoirs, there comes a new picture of a figure who still has an importance, not just to like-minded members of his church, but to all who are looking today for a Church renewed by Scripture. The Dictionary of National Biography rightly calls him "the strongest and not the least liberal" among the evangelicals of his day; but his successor at Liverpool, F.J. Chavasse, summed him up more strikingly: "A man of granite with the heart of a child."

Timothy Dudley-Smith

# PREFACE

The first generation of Evangelicals in the spiritual awakening under Whitefield and the Wesleys was a close-knit band of brothers who shared the same concern for the Gospel but were widely scattered in their spheres of activity. The next generation had strong focal points at Cambridge under Simeon and at Clapham under Wilberforce, and its leaders were great both in character and in achievement. E.L. Woodward believed that this movement had reached its real climax before the year 1815, but that it still represented the most active party in the Church of England.[1]

The third generation produced fewer men of outstanding quality, but there was a rapid growth in its rank and file. Lord Ashley, who in 1851 became the seventh Earl of Shaftesbury, was their greatest scion; he continued the tradition of public and political service, and his strong faith heightened his strong sense of duty.

Josiah Pratt, Edward Bickersteth and Henry Venn the younger may have been less widely influential than the leaders of a generation before, but they represented a fine pattern of true Evangelical continuity. They stood for the ideal of a "strict and pious life in an age of low moral standards. They maintained a serious and unselfish attitude towards public affairs. They used their wealth conscientiously, and on the whole to good and noble purpose. They cared nothing for popularity; their doctrines taught them at all times to save souls, and they preached as much by example as by exhortation."[2]

This was no less true at the height of Queen Victoria's

England when the continuity of the Evangelical cause was predominant in middle-class society. R.K. Ensor declared that its "remarkable feature was that it came so largely to dispense with the abnormal; made other-worldliness an everyday conviction and so to say a business proposition; and thus induced a highly civilised people to put pleasure in the background, and what it conceived to be duty in the foreground, and to a quite exceptional degree."[3] It was only when the laxer standards of the Prince of Wales and his friends began to infiltrate society that high spiritual ideals began to lose their hold.[4] But neither adversity nor obscurity were to destroy the strong pattern of Evangelical continuity.

The first authentic element in such Evangelical continuity is the fact that our faith sinks its roots in Christian history: it is nothing if not historical in its descent from the New Testament. The words of the psalmist may rightly be employed by each generation as it recalls the past: "We have heard with our ears, O God, our fathers have told us, what work Thou didst in their days, in the times of old" (Ps. 44:1).

Our faith does not date from the days of Simeon and Wilberforce whose wide spiritual vision helped to found the modern missionary movement, nor from the days of Wesley and Whitefield whose great moral courage helped to change the face of England. It is older than the age of Bunyan and Baxter when sturdy Puritans were willing to endure fines and imprisonment in the cause of spiritual freedom; it is older than the age of Ridley and Cranmer when earnest Reformers were ready to submit to the ordeal of fire so that they might light such a candle as by God's grace shall not go out. It is older than Wycliffe; it is older than Anselm; it is older than Aidan: it can be traced back through all the ages to its primitive origin in the revelation of the Gospel of the Lord Christ Himself.

Thus we claim that Evangelical continuity reaches right back beyond the martyrs of the Reformation, beyond the schoolmen of the Middle Ages, beyond the fathers of the first four Christian centuries, and that it took its rise when "the bright and morning star" first began to shine (Rev.

22:16). We may like to think of Irenaeus at the feet of Polycarp, and Polycarp at the feet of John the Divine; but we claim the right to sit with all three at the feet of Jesus Himself. We are taught in the school of Christ no less than were the Twelve, and ours is a benediction in which even they could not share: "Blessed are they that have not seen, and yet have believed" (John 20:29). We may dwell in spirit at the feet of Jesus and hear His Word, and this assures our place in the line of succession from the apostles.

This is not a gift which depends on the imposition of human hands; it owes all its reality to the experience of divine grace. It spells itself out in steadfast continuance "in the apostles' doctrine and fellowship, and in breaking of bread, and in prayers" (Acts 2:42). All that is of value in centuries of tradition we dare to claim as ours; it is at the heart of all true Evangelical continuity.

This is the answer to those who dismiss Evangelical testimony with the reproach of novelty in the march of time. We are residuary legatees of the great heritage of the New Testament, for we have been put in trust with the truth which has now been finally committed to the people of God (Jude 3).

There have been times in the course of Christian history when the fires of faith and vision seem to have been little more than dying embers; but the fire has never gone out, and the historic succession has never failed. It has pleased God time and again to fan that fire into fresh flame and to revive the Church where it was weak and in distress. There was little earthly prospect for the disciples in the catacombs of Rome or the refugees from the dragonnades of France; there was perhaps even less for Athanasius who dared to stand alone against the world or for Martin Luther who went to Worms though all the fiends of hell were there. But "if God be for us, who can be against us?" (Rom. 8:31).

We now live in an age when the creeds of secular survival have the world by the throat, and this is not unconnected with the fact that two wars have swept the world in a single generation; but we are the heirs and trustees of a spiritual inheritance which lifts men's eyes beyond the change and flux of time to that kingdom which shall never be moved.

The next authentic element in such Evangelical continuity is the fact that our faith draws its strength from recognised scholarship: it is nothing if not reasonable in its approach to the New Testament. St. Paul's charge to Timothy may rightly be applied to each generation as it confronts this fact: "I put thee in remembrance that thou stir up the gift of God, which is in thee ... for God hath not given us the spirit of fear; but of power, and of love, and of a sound mind" (2 Tim. 1:6-7).

There is no real conflict between Faith and Reason, for in the last analysis, what is Faith and what is Reason? Emil Brunner summed up his own reply to that question in one short pregnant sentence: "Faith is Reason, healed through the Word of God." It has always been the duty of Faith to walk hand in hand with Reason as far as Reason can go. Faith must then go where Reason cannot go; but not where it would be unreasonable to go. Faith may have to transcend Reason; it must never deny Reason. The last step which Reason itself can take is to confess that there is an infinitude of things beyond its grasp; then it becomes like a signpost on the path which Faith must follow.

Thus a reasonable faith becomes a moral necessity unless we are to walk blindfold through the darkness. This was clearly perceived by the apostolic writers, and the exhortation to the primitive disciples still stands: "Sanctify the Lord God in your hearts: and be ready always to give an answer to every man that asketh you a reason of the hope that is in you" (1 Pet. 3:15).

A wise Evangelical will always be strongly convinced of the necessity for clear thinking in doctrine and dogma. Today he is the man of yesterday's thinking, and tomorrow he will be the man of today's. The man who says that it does not matter what he thinks so long as he lives a good life has never faced the issue. This was expressed in the Book of Proverbs with perfect insight long ago: "As he thinketh in his heart, so is he" (Prov. 23:7).

There is greater need than ever for clear Bible teaching and sound theology in this age of meteoric progress in so many other fields of knowledge. Long and patient study lends new lustre to the unique value of the Scriptures as a divine revelation of truth, for the wisdom of the ages in the Word of God is vastly superior to the brilliance of the moment in the changing moods of human philosophy.

This is the answer to those who dismiss Evangelical testimony with the reproach of poverty in the realm of thought. Faith has nothing to fear and much to gain from all forms of learning, and it may not be too strong a claim to say that Evangelicals owe more to the search for truth than any other party within the Church. It has always been to their loss when they have felt tempted to neglect or ignore the progress of learning.

The powers of faith should be commensurate with the facts of knowledge, and faith should stretch itself to stand level with the growth of understanding. The great theologians who have left their mark on future generations have all been men of the highest mental calibre; it would not be easy to name any three men who have surpassed St. Paul, or Augustine, or John Calvin, in intellect and genius.

It was on the spring-tide of New Learning that the Reformation swept through Europe, and its impact was swiftest and surest in university circles. It was clearly seen that there can be no schism in Truth, and that knowledge in all its forms is the servant of true theology. Therefore we are bound to welcome the progress of learning in all its fields: in textual criticism as well as in historical research; in nuclear physics as well as in political science; and we are bound to do this just because we are bound to love the Lord our God with all our heart and with all our mind.

The third authentic element in such Evangelical continuity is the fact that our faith proves its worth in personal devotion: it is nothing if not spiritual in its response to the New Testament. It lays to heart the words of its Divine Master spoken on the eve of His death: "This is life eternal, that they might know Thee, the only true God, and Jesus

Christ whom Thou hast sent" (John 17:3).

The word "Christian" was coined by the wits of Antioch as a nickname for those who were known as Christ's men. Similar epithets such as "Protestant" or "Puritan" or "Methodist" came into vogue at various points of history as jibes at men whose faith was in earnest. It is hard to tell when the word "Evangelical" first came into such use, but its meaning is stamped on its surface in a way which none can mistake. It is a word which speaks of a definite Evangel; good news from God for all mankind.

This means that it insists on the realities of sin and of judgement; on our desperate impotence to save ourselves, and God's generous provision to meet our need; on the mercies offered in grace and the blessings received by faith; on a life of sonship and the hope of glory. All the virtues of the finest culture lose their truest value when the inmost spirit fails to vibrate beneath the touch of this glorious Evangel.

This is why our primary emphasis must rest on the needs of the soul. "There is none other name under heaven given among men, whereby we must be saved" (Acts 4:12). We cannot be content with a system of dogma or a routine of worship; these may be as cold and lifeless as a marble statue.

The Rev. Dr. Alan Cole in 1956 placed his finger on this problem in a searching remark. "I constantly dread for us all", he said, "what I have seen in some, an intellectual development that outstrips the spiritual development, and a spiritual insight that is not matched by the moral strength that alone leads to spiritual progress."

Our faith demands a deep response within the soul in the way of self-discipline, personal devotion, and true missionary-hearted service. The love of Christ constrains us to seek to confront men with that Name which is above all names, for we believe that the only hope for the world is to be found in Him. It is this hope which has inspired the Church with its martyr-witness down the ages; the world itself cannot ignore men who have been willing to pass through flood and fire for Him who is All in all.

This is the answer to those who dismiss Evangelical

testimony with the reproach of apathy in the face of need. It is hard to avoid the charge that many Evangelicals are a trifle withdrawn from the world to which they belong; they are aloof from the needs and problems of their neighbours; they contrive to enjoy a self-imposed isolation in the midst of modern society. But the Gospel is poles apart from such escapism and we cannot afford to live like social hermits in our own private dream-world.

Kathleen Heasman has furnished an excellent correction to such faulty thinking in her account of "Evangelicals In Action" in the Victorian era. We have been saved to serve and made to give, and our lives fail in their purpose if they are not poured out for God and spent for man. A pebble which absorbs all the rays of sunlight which fall upon it may be of little value; a diamond which drinks in those rays only to flash them out through every facet is of great worth. The first law of nature is that of self-preservation, but the first law of grace is that of self-sacrifice. "Whosoever will save his life shall lose it: but whosoever will lose his life for My sake, the same shall save it" (Luke 9:24). It is only when Christ fills the vision that the idea of sacrifice can disappear from man's limited horizon.

The chapters which follow tell the story of a man whose life and character exemplify the truth and strength of such Evangelical continuity. The life of John Charles Ryle was to stretch from the year after Waterloo to the dawn of the twentieth century. During that long lifetime, England would change; the Church would change; the world would change; and the degree of change would be almost beyond recognition. But the God of all grace and the good news of His love did not change, and the basic facts of Evangelical continuity were as real as ever.

Ryle's life was to witness the rise of the Oxford Movement and the spread of Higher Criticism; it saw the birth of the Keswick Movement and the growth of missionary effort. The stock from which he sprang would add strength and fibre to his spiritual inheritance and would help to fit him to stand in the forefront of the battle in his day and generation.

Edward Irving in an early sermon for the London Missionary Society drew the picture of an apostolic servant of the Gospel in bold colours:

> A man of sublime and dominant faith; a man without purse, without a change of raiment, without a staff; without the care of making or keeping friends; without the desire of worldly gain, without the apprehension of worldly loss; without the care of life, without the fear of death; of no rank, of no country; a man of one thought – the Gospel of Christ; and a man of one purpose – the glory of God; a fool, and content to be reckoned a fool for Christ; a madman, and content to be reckoned a madman for Christ.[5]

Does this exaggerate? Does it suggest reckless austerity? Must a modern servant of Christ be just like this? Outward details may change, but the spirit remains; and it has been the strength of true Evangelical continuity that the Church has never wanted some who really answer the spirit of this luminous description.

# JOHN CHARLES RYLE

## 1816-1900

O good grey head which all men knew,
O voice from which their omens all men drew,
O iron nerve to true occasion true,
O fall'n at length that tower of strength
Which stood four-square to all the winds that blew.

*Alfred Lord Tennyson (1852)*

# ETON AND OXFORD: 1816-1837

John Charles Ryle was born at Park House, Macclesfield, on May 10th, 1816, the fourth of six children and the elder of two brothers. The Ryles traced their descent from a yeoman family whose first known forbear died in 1609; they had long been established in the beautiful countryside of Cheshire. "Macclesfield lies in the shadow of the Peak District"[1] and had been the centre of a flourishing industry in the silk trade since the sixteenth century.

Ryle's grandfather, John Ryle, had made a large fortune in the course of that trade and had become a substantial property owner. He died before Ryle was born and Ryle could only write of him in brief terms: "I only know he was a very good man and an earnest Christian, and an intimate friend of the famous John Wesley, who frequently came to stay at his house; and who mentions him in his journals."[2]

Wesley's first visit to Macclesfield was in 1748, and he was to return at regular intervals right up to 1790 within a year of his death. John Ryle had become a convert as a result of that first visit and was to prove a staunch friend of Wesley throughout his life. He remained a faithful member of the Church of England, but he encouraged the Methodists with generous support in public and in private. He made available a site for a meeting-house in 1764 and for a chapel in 1780. A new chapel had to be built eight years later and Ryle gave a thousand pounds to help meet the cost.

He had served as mayor of Macclesfield and his integrity as a Christian gentleman had been evident to all. When he died in 1808, his large fortune was left to his son, John; but of far more significance was that intangible inheritance which was derived from a lifetime of faith and strong Christian character.

John Ryle was married to Susanna, a cousin of Sir Richard Arkwright, and had made his home at Park House which had been built by his father at the same time as a silk mill. He became Mayor of Macclesfield in 1809, and his fortune steadily expanded during the following years. He enjoyed an income of something between fifteen and twenty thousand pounds per annum, and he became well known as a banker and a landed proprietor.

It is not known to what extent he shared the strong Christian convictions of his father. He seems to have had a nominal connection with Christ Church which had been built during his father's lifetime as an Evangelical foundation.[3] John Charles Ryle was to say of him: "Poor dear man! ... he came into his fortune too soon and left the Wesleyans and got thrown into the company of men who did him no good. But I always think that he secretly remembered what he used to hear when he was a boy and knew more about religion than he cared to confess or practise."[4] Nevertheless it is interesting to note that both John Ryle's sons were ordained and that two of his daughters married clergymen.

Park House was a home marked by wealth and ease; the Ryles grew up surrounded with luxury. John Ryle was too absorbed in his business affairs to take any notice of them and it was left to their mother to fuss over their health and dress and manners in general. But John Ryle had a yacht called the *Seaflower*, and he used to take his family to Bridlington for holidays in the summer. Once at least he took them all to Crosby for the sake of his daughter's health, and once to Hastings for his wife's health. The best remembered occasions were picnics on Flamborough Head "and the smell of turnip fields on top of the cliffs".[5]

John Charles Ryle did not have much to record about his first eight years. "They were happy and pretty harmless years," he wrote, "although destitute of any real religion. We had few cares, no sickness, no death, no anxieties, and wanted for nothing. We might have been better done for, and we might have been worse."[6]

He could read well at the age of four and could always be kept quiet with a book. Every morning the clerk of St. Michael's Church, Isaac Eaton, came for an hour and a half to teach him "to read, write, and cipher,"[7] and his sister's governess taught him the rudiments of Latin.

Then, in August 1824, school life began when he was eight years old, "too early", so he would later reflect, " ... by at least two years".[8] He was sent to a small private school kept by the Rev. John Jackson, first at Bowdon, then at Over, a small village near Nantwich some twenty miles away. Jackson was well thought of and his school had boys from all the leading families in Cheshire.

Ryle thought it was "a good school for learning, but very rough so far as the comfort of the boys was concerned".[9] There were sixteen boys at the time, and they slept in two rooms; there was a good deal of horse-play, and he was not at all happy. "I don't think I was an ill-natured, bad-tempered boy," he wrote, "but I was sturdy, very independent and combative. I had a very strong opinion of my own, and never cared a bit for being in a minority, and was ready to fight anybody however big if necessary."[10]

So the man he was to become had its deeper-seated roots in his childhood; but he was glad enough when the time came to leave. "I left Mr. Jackson's school in December 1827," he went on to record, "tolerably well grounded in Latin and Greek, but having learned a vast amount of moral evil and got no moral good."[11]

Ryle went on to Eton where his name was enrolled on February 7th, 1828, and where he soon had his feet on the rungs of a brilliant career. He was eleven years old, and the next six and three-quarter years were spent at Eton.

The headmaster was Dr. John Keate who had held that

appointment since 1809; his last seven years in office coincided with Ryle's years at the school. Ryle was subsequently to say that Keate was "a good disciplinarian, a good scholar, and kept good order", but that "he was a thorough Tory of the old school and of the worst sort, and set his face steadfastly against any sort of reform or any effort to meet the times."[12] He thought that the provost and most of the fellows were "old fossils ... utterly unable to see the necessity of changes."[13]

All this made him more than thankful that he was placed in Hawtrey's house where in point of comfort he had all that he could desire: "We were well fed, well cared for, and wanted for nothing."[14] But there was more, much more, than that. Edward Craven Hawtrey inspired him with the most favourable recollection as a tutor who took great pains with boys who were disposed to read.

Ryle felt awkward enough in his first six months at the school, but found his place as time went on. His work improved as he went up the school and he rose to the top of his class when he passed into the fifth form. Hawtrey taught him to broaden his studies beyond the narrow circle of Greek and Latin authors, and he began to read widely in French and English literature as well as in Greek and Roman history. "Under his guidance," Ryle recalled in 1890, "I read privately nearly all the books in which I was finally examined at Oxford."[15] Strange as it seems today, he learned nothing of arithmetic or mathematics in those seven years at Eton; but in his final year at school, he was "very high" in his place in the sixth form.[16]

When the Newcastle Scholarship was founded in 1829, it soon became one of the most coveted distinctions; it was indeed the blue riband of classical attainment at Eton at the time when Ryle's son, Herbert, was placed first in 1875.[17] Ryle sat for the Newcastle Scholarship in his own day and, so he wrote, "surprised everyone by the position which I took".[18] The *Memoir of Herbert Ryle* states that he took third place, but in his fragment of autobiography, Ryle said that he only came fourth in his final attempt.[19]

It had another importance because it made divinity for the first time a school subject in its own right and with its own reward. This proved to be of the greatest moment for Ryle, for it helped to mould his mind and outlook. "Most boys," wrote Ryle, "knew far more about the heathen gods and goddesses than about Jesus Christ."[20] But the Newcastle Scholarship turned his thoughts in another direction. "It is a simple fact," he wrote long afterwards, "that the beginning of any clear doctrinal views I have ever attained myself was reading up the Articles at Eton for the Newcastle Scholarship ... I shall always thank God for what I learned then."[21]

But there were more general interests as well. He became a member of the Eton Society which had been founded in 1811 as a select social and debating body: it was nicknamed Pop and limited its membership to twenty-five boys. It used to meet every Saturday afternoon in the Reading Room at Hutton's shop and Ryle took a leading part in its affairs. Speeches were all taken down and preserved in the Old Chronicles of the Society. W.E. Gladstone and Lord Derby had been active participants not many years before. But Ryle was too active to confine himself to reading and the Eton Society; he was always fond of outdoor pursuits and games. One whole summer he spent all his spare time on the river and he was an ardent hockey player; but the game which he loved above all was cricket.

"Nothing did I enjoy so much as cricket when I was in the XI," he wrote, "and as long as I live I think I shall say that the happiest days I ever spent in a simple, earthly way were the days when I was captain of the XI in Eton playing-fields."[22] He played in the matches against Harrow and Winchester both in 1833 and in 1834. His highest score was twenty-six, and his average for eight innings was only eleven. He won a place in the University XI in his first year at Oxford and in later life he was to record that he captained the side in his last two seasons.[23]

The match against Cambridge first took place in 1827, but did not become a regular fixture until 1836. Ryle had much to do with this through contacts with old Etonians who were then at Cambridge.[24] The *Memoir of Herbert Ryle* notes that in the match of 1836, Ryle took ten wickets.[25] Cricket never lost its appeal for him, although like Henry Venn the elder, he gave up playing once he was ordained.[26]

He watched the fortunes of Eton and Oxford with unflagging interest to the end of his life. "I am very glad that you are not giving up cricket," he told one of his sons in May 1876. "Take my word for it, the time is not wasted."[27] And in 1886 he added a postscript to a letter, expressing amazement at the defeat of Cambridge and delight at Eton's triumph over Harrow. "I had begun to think," he wrote, "they would never win again."[28] The veteran is overheard once more a year or two later in his advice for a youthful grandson: "You may tell him from me that he will never make a good batter unless he learns to bring forward his left shoulder and play with a straight bat. The last innings I ever got was at Lincoln when I got eighty-eight runs not out, and played with left shoulder forward the whole time."[29]

Ryle believed that cricket had been of great value to him because it had helped to develop all his latent gifts for leadership. "It gave me a power of commanding, managing, organising and directing, seeing through men's capacities and using every man in the post to which he is best suited, bearing and forbearing, keeping men around me in good temper, which I have found of infinite use on lots of occasions in life, though in very different matters."[30]

"In October 1834, I entered Christ Church, Oxford, and remained there exactly three years."[31] William Tuckwell, looking back from the end of the century, thought Oxford in the thirties had never been more beautiful or so attractive.

The approach ... by the Henley Road was the most beautiful in the world. Soon after passing Littlemore you came in sight of, and did not lose again, the sweet city with its dreaming spires, driven along a road now crowded and obscured with dwellings, open then to cornfields on the right, to undisclosed meadows on the left, with an unbroken view of the long line of towers, rising out of foliage less high and veiling than after sixty more years of growth today. At once, without suburban interval, you entered the finest quarter of the town, rolling under Magdalen Tower and past the Magdalen elms, then in full unmutilated luxuriance, till the exquisite curves of the High Street opened on you, as you drew up at the Angel or passed on to the Mitre and the Star.[32]

But the Oxford of the thirties was still governed by statutes which dated back to Archbishop Laud, and any movement for reform was subject to bitter controversy. "The Colleges were independent societies jealous of outside interference; the governing body in each University" (Oxford and Cambridge) "was composed mainly of heads of houses, elderly and safe men who did not wish for change, and the clerical vote was always in a majority in the general assemblies of the masters of arts."[33]

Oxford, like Cambridge, was the training ground for clergy in the Church of England, and no one could matriculate unless he had subscribed to the Thirty-Nine Articles. As a result, criticism turned as much on religious exclusiveness as on academic shortcomings, and this made it easy for the College heads and fellows to argue that any movement for reform was part of a larger attack on the Church of England.[34]

Ryle went up to Oxford at a time when Oriel was being displaced by Balliol as the leading College in the field of academic honours, but Christ Church was not far behind. Christ Church had been founded by Wolsey in 1525 and at first had been known as Cardinal College. It was dominated by the Tom Tower which housed Great Tom, the huge bell which rang out one hundred and one strokes every evening at five minutes past nine.

Hobhouse had a happy comment on all this in his book,

*Oxford As It Was And Is Today:* "The tolling of Great Tom is like a symbol of the predominance of Christ Church over the University. It is easily the most important, the most delightful of all Oxford's foundations. It has the largest revenue, it provides the best food and the most spacious rooms, and it sends forth the most successful alumni of any College."[35]

Certainly it produced a remarkable group of gifted graduates in the twenties and thirties of the nineteenth century: the list includes Edward Bouverie Pusey, William Ewart Gladstone, Charles Wordsworth and Charles Canning. In the years from 1831 to 1835, some thirty Christ Church men took first-class degrees; this was at a time when the average first-class list, issued twice a year, rarely exceeded a dozen names from all Colleges.[36]

The dean when Ryle went up was Thomas Gaisford who held office from 1831 to 1855. Ryle's first tutor was Augustus Short, a rather dull High Churchman who later became the first Bishop of Adelaide. "Short as a tutor was perfectly useless," Ryle observed, "and I never learned anything from him."[37] To Ryle's relief, Short left Christ Church towards the end of 1835 and was replaced by Henry Liddell who with Robert Scott was to compile the famous Liddell and Scott Lexicon. Ryle wrote of him without reserve: "Liddell was a very good tutor and I heartily wish I had been under him during the whole time I was at Oxford."[38]

Ryle took a strong dislike to the tone of society which he found in Oxford. "The buildings and colleges," he wrote, "are things matchless in the world, and to talk of comparing Oxford and Cambridge is simply ridiculous. But I thoroughly disliked the tone of society among the undergraduates at Oxford, the more so from its complete unlikeness to what I had been used to at Eton."[39] He felt there was too much fawning upon wealth and title, and this induced a coldness and distance and a want of sociable goodwill.

His outlet was cricket; but apart from cricket, he does

not seem to have been drawn into undergraduate interests or activities.

He had entered Christ Church less than twelve months after Keble had preached the famous assize sermon which is commonly regarded as having launched the Oxford Movement, and the Oxford in which he lived was to seethe with ferment as the *Tracts for the Times* began to appear. He must have been aware of the storm of controversy which was evoked by the Tractarians, but he never felt the magnetic influence which John Henry Newman was able to exert in so many quarters. He was too masculine in mind and character to fall under the spell of a Catholic revival.

He felt that his first two years were practically thrown away, and it was not until Liddell took him in hand that he began to stretch his mind and make full use of his talents. Nevertheless at the end of his first year, he won a Fell Exhibition in his own College; at the end of his second year, he won the Craven University Scholarship; and at the end of the third year, he took so brilliant a first in Greats, the Literae Humaniores, that it was said that the examiners might well have placed him with Arthur Stanley and Henry Highton in a class by themselves.[40] He took his degree with first-class honours in 1837, but did not proceed to his master's degree until 1871.[41] The last honour conferred on him by his Alma Mater was the award by diploma of a Doctorate of Divinity in May 1880.

Ryle was indeed a young man of remarkable promise with his academic honours, his cricket renown and his tall and striking figure; but beneath the surface, there were other factors at work, and they were to have a still more profound effect on his development.

His last year at Oxford was to see a change in his life which was fraught with deeper issues than he could have foreseen. His home was one in which respectable standards had always been maintained, but it had been lacking in spiritual vitality. A large income and a country estate had helped the Ryles to fold their arms and dwell at ease in the lap of plenty. Macclesfield had only two churches for a population of thirty-five thousand people, and they were served by men whom he later described as "high and dry sticks of the old school".[42]

When he came to look back on his life through the calm eyes of the late fifties, he could only say that he had grown up with no real faith at all. He did not know what came first or what last in the economy of truth, and what he did know had no clear order and no vital priority.[43] "I certainly never said my prayers," he wrote, "or read a word of my Bible, from the time I was seven to the time I was twenty-one."[44] He had no taste for the wilder frivolities of youth, and had gone through Oxford with a stainless reputation like the rich young ruler; but he had felt no sense of guilt or need, and was simply content to live without thought or care for the things of God. He had crammed his mind with the facts of the Gospel in his reading for the Newcastle Scholarship, but he had yet to feel the touch of God's finger in a way that would turn such facts into living reality.

The means by which he was aroused from this spiritual indifference were at first more or less insensible, but there was a controlling providence which led him step by step towards the goal of true personal conversion.

Perhaps the situation in Macclesfield was not as dark as he supposed. John Bird Sumner had become Bishop of Chester in 1828, one of the earliest Evangelicals to be consecrated. A new church, St. George's Sutton, had been opened in Macclesfield in 1828 and was consecrated in 1834.

The Rev. John Burnet was appointed as its minister in July that year and his faithful preaching of the Gospel soon led to the conversion of Ryle's cousin, Harry Arkwright, and then of his sister, Susan. "There was a kind of stir among dry bones" as the congregation felt the breath of fresh and fervent preaching, and Ryle was not left in the dark where such news was concerned. It made him think, although there was no real change in his life at the time.[45]

His first serious conviction of sin came soon after he left Eton when his friend, Algernon Coote, rebuked him for swearing: "he was the first person who ever told me to think, repent, and pray."[46] Ryle was startled; he never swore again. Two years went by; then in mid-summer 1837, not long before his final examinations, he fell ill with severe inflammation of the chest. "That was the time," he wrote, "when I distinctly remember I began to read my Bible and began to pray."[47]

Ryle knew that those examinations would tax his mind and strength to the limit. He had to be ready to take a test in no less than sixteen Greek and Latin authors, and there would be papers on several other subjects as well. Written tests would take up five days, and would then be followed by a final day of oral examination before an audience of tutors and undergraduates. It was indeed a formidable prospect, especially when he was ill. But the hand of God was on him, and that divine hold was never to be relaxed. Ryle shook off the illness, but could not shake himself free from the grasp of that strong hand.

What happened next? Ryle's own record of his conversion is marked by an unwonted reticence. He said no more than that "from mid-summer 1837 till Christmas in the same year" was the turning point in his life.[48] That short illness and the approach of his final examinations had left him not a little depressed; but the crisis of his soul was at hand.

It came when he sauntered into church one Sunday after the service had begun; he was so far oblivious of the world at large that he could never recall which church it was. The prayers were read by a stranger, and he forgot the text of the sermon; but his soul was seized by the grace of God and his hidden anxieties were once and for all put to flight.

It was in the reading of the second lesson that God spoke to his heart. That lesson was taken from the second chapter in the Epistle to the Ephesians: the great passage in which St. Paul proclaimed as a sober reality the true saving strength and virtue of grace. It was read with uncommon earnestness; two verses in particular were read with an impressive emphasis. There was a pause between each phrase, as though to let each new concept sink down into the mind: "For by grace ... are ye saved ... through faith; ... and that, not of yourselves; ... it is the gift of God; ... not of works ... lest any man should boast" (Eph. 2:8-9).

Ryle must have heard those words often enough before, but their point had been dulled by the confused murmur of the world all around. But that morning, in the silence of each fresh pause, the still small voice of God was heard; that voice spoke to his heart in a way that awoke the power of faith with an immediate response to the grace and mercy of God. It was in the simple hearing of those words of Scripture that he grasped the secret of the Gospel, and that sudden discovery of the meaning of the grace of God was to make him a new man in a new world.

Ryle's *Self-Portrait* did not record any of these details, but the facts were well known. Alfred Christopher was the incumbent of St. Aldate's Church in Oxford from 1859-1905; he confirmed this account in an article which appeared in *The Record* during the week after Ryle's death.[49] W.H. Griffith Thomas was a curate at St. Aldate's from 1889-1896; he was in the best possible position to learn the truth and he placed it on record as a remarkable instance of the converting majesty of the Holy Spirit through a single text of Scripture.[50] J.W. Diggle, who lectured at Merton in 1870 and afterwards became Bishop of Carlisle, told his ordinands in 1902: "Bishop Ryle owed his conversion to the reading of a lesson in church."[51]

Ryle himself was content to note that his character underwent a complete and profound alteration; the change was so great that it had the most sweeping effects on his whole life and on all his future.[52] Ryle owed nothing to the Tractarian Movement which was making Oxford ring with the strife of tongues; but he knew that he could never repay his debt to the mercy of God, and this experience, based on this text, gave him a lifelong love for the wholesome doctrines of grace.

It was the year of the Queen's accession, and his life was to stretch almost to the close of her reign. He was on the threshold of his career as a Victorian of the Victorians, and it was of singular importance that this change took place when it did. It was just in time to allow him to work out his own firm and decided convictions before he went down from Oxford. He could say that by the end of that year (1837) he was "fairly launched as a Christian" and he never looked back.[53] He was ready to take his place as an established Christian in the new world which the new reign had just brought in.

Ryle's main concern in the narrative of his conversion was to impress on his children the great salient convictions which took hold on his mind and were to shape his life from that time forward. There were certain truths which flashed their light on his mind "as clearly and sharply as the picture on a photographic plate when the developing liquid is poured".[54] What were these truths?

> The extreme sinfulness of sin and my own personal sinfulness; the entire suitableness of the Lord Jesus Christ by His sacrifice, substitution and intercession to be the Saviour of the sinner's soul; the absolute necessity of anybody who would be saved being born again or converted by the Holy Ghost; the indispensable necessity of holiness of life, being the only evidence of a true Christian; the absolute need of coming out from the world and being separate from its vain customs, recreations, and standards of what is right, as well as from its sins; the supremacy of the Bible as the only rule of what is true in faith or right in practice, and the need of regular study and reading it; the absolute necessity of daily private prayer and communion with God ...[55]

Ryle said that all these great primary convictions grew up in his mind before the end of 1837; nothing he could recall in later life seemed to him to be so clear and distinct. "People may account for such a change as they like; my own belief is that no real rational explanation of it can be given but that of the Bible; it was what the Bible calls conversion or regeneration. Before that time I was dead in sins and on the high road to hell, and from that time I have become alive and had a hope of heaven. And nothing to my mind can account for it but the free, sovereign grace of God."[56] His mind had been made up; the die was cast: for the Christ who was now in him was the hope of glory.

# WINCHESTER AND HELMINGHAM:
## 1837-1861

Ryle was as glad to leave Oxford as he had been sorry to leave Eton. He had declined proposals to submit himself for election as a student at Christ Church or a fellow at Balliol or Brasenose. He was by nature a man of affairs rather than an academic and he returned home to equip himself for a life of public activity.

He read law for six months and then joined his father's banking business to gain further experience. He held a commission in the Cheshire Yeomanry and he became a county magistrate. He was asked to stay at many leading houses in the county, for he was known as a highly eligible young man who was certain to make a mark. Erstwhile pleasures of a worldly nature had dropped away; the billiards and dancing which had taken up so much of his time in his earlier vacations had now come to an end. "Cricket," he wrote, "was the one amusement which I never gave up after I became a Christian, so long as I was a layman."[1]

But the great change in his life was hardly welcome at home. It led to an awkwardness and a sense of estrangement in his own family; it drove a wedge between him and old friends. They thought him wrong and he thought they were wrong; they were annoyed with him, and he was sorry for them. They may have said little, but their perplexity was all too plain. This only tended to increase his feeling of isolation and the three and a half years after he left Oxford were for him years of constant trial and difficulty.

But there were gains as well and he was soon at home in new circles with new friendships. Thus, for example, he often went to Lansdowne House at Leamington where William Marsh and his daughter, Catherine, were then living, and he was to say as late as 1895 that the recollection of the pleasant evenings under their roof was as green as ever.[2]

John Ryle had won a seat in the House of Commons in 1833 as the first member for the borough of Macclesfield and he held this seat until 1837. This was the year in which he gave up Park House and bought the beautiful estate of Henbury. This was about three miles west of Macclesfield and it consisted of about a thousand acres. "The house, woods, and water were out of all proportion to the size of the estate, and made it a very desirable residence."[3]

Thus when Ryle left Oxford, Henbury became his home, and he fell in love with it all. But he felt that he was hardly more than "a tolerated person" at home. As a result, he was thrown back on books and he read as widely as he could with an eye to the future. He was especially impressed with Wilberforce's *Practical View of Christianity* and John Newton's *Cardiphonia*. He used to take prayers before breakfast for his sisters and the housekeeper and her maid, but his parents would not attend. He felt inhibited while he remained under their roof; nevertheless he was often asked to speak at religious gatherings.

It was his aim to win a seat in the House of Commons like his father, and he was a frequent speaker on the political platform as a Tory. One newspaper report of a meeting in Macclesfield said that he had spoken "with much ability... and at great length".[4]

It is not hard to form a clear mental image of Ryle during those years. He was in his early twenties, gifted and good-looking, secure in his knowledge of the Gospel, welcome among those who were like-minded, always happy on the cricket field, yet not at ease in his own home or among many of his old friends. But in calm retrospect, he came to see how God was fitting him for after-work in a way he did not know. "I was training much and learning much in passing through a school of experience which afterwards was very useful to me."[5]

But all his dreams were dashed to dust by the sudden total collapse of his father's business affairs. The silk trade had been in decline towards the end of the thirties, and this had been a cause of some anxiety. But it was a bank crash in June 1841 that wrecked John Ryle's fortune and dragged him down into swift and total ruin.

John Ryle's father had joined with a fellow silk manufacturer named Daintry to take over the bank owned by Hawkins and Mills when it failed in 1800. It had prospered until John Ryle agreed to establish a branch at Manchester. This in itself was a mistake, but what made it much worse was the fact that neither Ryle nor Daintry gave it their own personal oversight. They left it in the hands of a manager and do not seem to have known his fatal lack of competence. The funds of the bank were squandered by loans and advances to all sorts of people "who ought never to have had a penny".[6]

When a run on the bank began in June 1841, the London banker with whom Ryle and Daintry corresponded stopped payment, and the banks at Macclesfield and Manchester were forced to follow suit. Ryle was bankrupt; "every single acre and penny my father possessed had to be given up to meet the demand of the creditors".[7]

John Ryle had to break up his household and dismiss his servants; he had to sell his home and all his assets; he had to go into obscurity and spend the rest of his life trying to settle his debts. John Charles Ryle felt a strong moral obligation to do what he could to help his father. For years he wore his clothes threadbare and used as much of his stipend as he could in order to help satisfy the just claims of creditors.[8] The last payment was made twenty years later in 1861, but for thirty years the memory was as bitter and painful as if it had been yesterday.[9]

This dire calamity fell on the Ryle household like an awful crash of thunder. The family was penniless except for the money settled on Mrs. Ryle at the time of her marriage. John

Charles Ryle would never forget the shock. "We got up one summer's morning with all the world before us as usual, and went to bed that same night completely and entirely ruined."[10]

Mrs. Ryle went to stay with her brother in London; Emma went to the New Forest; Frederick was on the Continent reading for a degree; Susan and Caroline were already married; John Charles and Mary Ann stayed on with their father for six weeks while he wound up his affairs.

Those six weeks were the most wretched that he ever had to pass through. He sold his two horses and his Yeomanry uniform; morning, noon, and night, he felt crushed by the thought that he was about to leave the home he loved.

Time would never erase from his mind the wrench of going away when the moment came in August. The whole estate was in the full charm of summer beauty, but to him it seemed as still and silent as a graveyard.

Nothing I think touched me that morning so much as the face of my old Lyme mastiff, Caesar, who was especially fond of me. I remember he looked at me as if he did not understand it, and could not see why he could not go with me too. Poor dog, for a whole month afterwards he made his way into the house every morning as soon as the doors were opened and went up to my room; there he lay at the door from morning till night and nothing would induce him to stir. When the sun went down in the evening and it became dark, he used to get up, smell at the bottom of the door, whine piteously and walk downstairs. This he repeated every day for a month. At last it affected the people who were left in the house so much that they could stand it no longer.[11]

He was given away, but did not live very long; Ryle never saw him again.

Ryle was twenty-five years old at the time when this magnificent inheritance was snatched away. His father and mother settled down at Anglesey opposite Ryde where they lived out the rest of their days. He spent three months as the guest of Colonel Thornhill in the New Forest while he pondered what he should do.

The ploughshare of adversity had cut a deep furrow in his inmost spirit; he felt as though he could hardly lift up his head.[12] But there can be no doubt that God used this calamity to turn his heart towards his true life-work, for the thought of ordination had not even crossed his mind as long as his hope for a political career had been practicable. He had felt no initial vocation to the Christian ministry, and his ultimate decision was a surprise. "I became a clergyman," he wrote, "because I felt shut up to do it and saw no other course of life open to me."[13]

An unexpected invitation to accept a title in the parish of Fawley in Hampshire made him think that God had cut him off from other prospects in order to direct his mind to this sacred calling. The news went round among his friends, and a letter to Catherine Marsh from Charlotte Leycester referred to it. "John Ryle will be ordained on December 12 and preaches his first sermon on the 19th," she wrote; "would your dear father remember him in prayer?"[14] Charles Richard Sumner ordained him at Farnham Castle on that December day in 1841, and he entered on his labours in a remote corner of the New Forest at Exbury.

A cure of souls in the south of England was a vast change from his lovely home in Cheshire; but hard work would help to heal his sense of hurt and disappointment. "I have not the least doubt it was all for the best," he would yet write. "If I had not been ruined, I should never have been a clergyman, never have preached a sermon, or written a tract or book."[15]

The Rev. W. Gibson was Ryle's first and only rector, and he was away in Malta for the greater part of Ryle's time in the parish. His chief claim to any kind of fame was the fact that he married first the daughter of John Bird Sumner, then the daughter of Charles Richard Sumner. He was very kind to Ryle when at home, but was ultra cautious in his church work: "so afraid of doing wrong that he would hardly do right."[16]

The parish of Fawley covered a large triangular piece of the New Forest lying between Southampton Water and the Solent. Ryle was responsible for the Chapel of Ease at Exbury with a district about three miles wide and two miles broad. It was "a poor rural parish", but it was here that he laid the foundations of his ministry.

He lived in the hamlet of Langley, half-way between Exbury and Fawley, and in the midst of a rough and neglected population. Many of them had been brought up as poachers and smugglers; they lived in such utter neglect of God that it seemed as if nothing could move them. He had to prepare two written sermons for every Sunday and two cottage lectures for Wednesdays and Thursdays; these were given in small crowded dwellings which reeked with the smoke from peat fires.

"Nobody ever told me what was right or wrong in the pulpit," he recalled in 1886; "the result was that the first year of my preaching was a series of experiments."[17] His own common sense soon taught him to avoid any language that was beyond his hearers and to cultivate a plain, strong and forceful simplicity. He went in and out of cottage homes with exemplary patience and the church was soon filled on Sundays. "I kept a regular account of all the families in the parish," he wrote, "and was in every house in the parish at least once a month."[18] Such a diligent ministry was not without reward. "I think they would have done anything for me, and I believe the influence I had among them was very great indeed."[19]

Typhus and scarlet fever were rife in the heaths and commons of that low-lying and ill-drained parish: Ryle was in great demand for the simple healing measures he could provide. But his own health broke down at the end of two years and he resigned from the curacy in November 1843. Bishop Sumner at once offered him the parish of St. Thomas, Winchester, and he entered on his ministry there in December. His house was small but good, and he settled down with one elderly woman servant, a boy and a dog. The church seated some six hundred people in old-fashioned pews; there were three thousand people in the parish. He preached morning and evening on Sundays, and began a week-day lecture in a school room. "I set to work tooth and nail," he wrote, "and having youth on my side and nothing but my work to think about, no wife or children at home, I soon filled my church to suffocation and turned the parish upside down."[20]

Residence in Winchester brought him into contact with Samuel Wilberforce who was the leading High Churchman in the diocese and was rector of Alverstoke which took in Anglesey where the Ryles lived. Wilberforce exercised a strong influence on the Ryle household. Frederick was his curate; Mary and Emma fell under his spell. Only John Ryle, true to his own early background, "remained impervious to his 'extremely pernicious' High Church teaching".[21]

Wilberforce often invited Ryle to preach at Alverstoke and sometimes attended Ryle's church in Winchester. "This lasted," so Ryle wrote, "till one memorable night when he had a long discussion with me till a late hour about baptismal regeneration, in which he tried hard to turn me from Evangelical views on that subject."[22] Ryle stood his ground, and the conversation had no effect.

But Ryle was still haunted by a sense of desperate poverty; he found it hard to live on a stipend of no more than one hundred pounds a year. He shrank as far as he could from social contact with well-to-do parishioners; he shrank as well from the society of eligible young ladies. It was awkward for a young and unmarried incumbent in a city like Winchester: so his enigmatic remarks affirmed.[23]

But he had not been more than five months in Winchester before the Lord Chancellor offered him the parish of Helmingham in Suffolk. This was worth no less than five hundred pounds a year and would make him independent at last. Therefore in May 1844, though not without regret, he left his parish in Winchester and moved to the diocese of Norwich where he was to spend the next thirty-six years.

Ryle's new church was on the fringe of the park lands which belonged to the Tollemache family at Helmingham

Hall. They claimed that they had held land in England since before 1066 as the couplet declares:

> When William the Conqueror reigned with great fame
> Bentley was my seat and Tollemache was my name.[24]

The Hall was built in the reign of Henry VIII, complete with moat and drawbridge, and the squire since 1840 was John Tollemache who had inherited immense landed wealth in Cheshire and in Suffolk. He sat in the House of Commons from 1841 to 1872, and was raised to the peerage in 1876 in recognition of his stature as a model landlord. He had a huge family and the size of his household was on a scale to fit his large ideas. There were butlers, valets, footmen, night watchmen, a steward, a groom of the chambers, and an incredible number of maids, who had to file into the Hall for prayers twice a day and attend church on Sundays in full livery.[25]

The rectory at Helmingham was in urgent need of repair; it was to take a year to put in order. During that time, Ryle was the guest of Mr. and Mrs. Tollemache in Helmingham Hall. He did not like such an arrangement, but was driven to accept their invitation from sheer necessity.

Tollemache had married Georgina Louisa Best in August 1826; she was a devout Evangelical. Ryle had come to know her soon after her conversion in 1837,[26] and he may have owed his appointment to her suggestion.

Tollemache himself spent most of his time in London, but when at home he filled the house with guests. There were seldom less than eighteen or twenty who sat down to dinner and Ryle soon came to know many of them. Among others whom he named with pleasure were the Hopes, the Harcourts, and Archbishop John Bird Sumner: "I always thank God that I met them and think their acquaintance did me good."[27] Nevertheless it was a great relief to him when he could move into the rectory in the summer of 1845; it stood next to the church, and he had a cook, a housemaid and a man who worked out of doors.

Then in July 1846 he sustained a grievous sorrow when Mrs. Tollemache died after an illness of only two or three hours. "To me it was an enormous loss," he wrote. "She was always most kind and friendly to me, and I believe really delighted in my ministry ... I take occasion to say that, taking her for all in all, she was the brightest example of a Christian woman I ever saw."[28]

Ryle would never forget the crowds that came for her funeral when it fell to him to preach the sermon. Her piety and devotion had matched her great beauty and her death was an irreparable loss for her husband. He would marry again and would father twenty-four sons and a daughter; but to Ryle, Helmingham was never the same place and Tollemache never the same man again.

Helmingham Hall was the focal point in the life of the parish in which there were only some three hundred people all told. It was a great contrast with the parish of three thousand from which Ryle had just come and he soon found that to visit the three hundred people who lived within a mile of the church on all sides was an easy matter.

The church itself dated from the fourteenth century and "was situated on the edge of the park, looking up a gentle slope to the Hall some six hundred yards away".[29] The church had been restored and was in perfect order, though cluttered with memorials of the Tollemache family. The squire owned every acre in the parish; the people were all his tenants; and his word was law. There was no village street, nor public house, nor shop; there was no village school until 1853.

Ryle went in and out of cottage homes in the same earnest spirit as in the New Forest and he gradually filled the church with a large congregation. "A visitor in 1858 counted some one hundred and sixty people crowded into the church and noted that the Rector preached for a long time and seemingly without notes."[30]

He soon came to know all the leading Evangelicals in the county and "commenced the habit of going about speaking and preaching in all directions".[31] This meant that he often had to drive an open carriage, even in the depth of winter, up to thirty miles in order to preach in lonely places; and he kept this up with little intermission throughout the seventeen years he spent at Helmingham.

He was always at home in the pulpit and on the platform, but he was thought distant and reserved because he shunned social activities. He had in fact found a better use for leisure. "I had more time for reading and thinking and storing my mind than I have ever had before or since."[32]

The time spent in reading proved to be the first step towards time for writing. His first ventures were as practical and as relevant from a parish point of view as he could make them. He had a great admiration for John Newton and the Olney Hymns which Newton and Cowper had composed for use at his mid-week meeting for prayer. This led him to compile a hymn book which was published in 1849 with the title *Spiritual Songs*, selected by J.C. Ryle. After several reprints, it was replaced in 1850 by *Hymns for the Church on Earth*, selected and arranged by J.C. Ryle. "I hold strongly," he wrote in the Preface, "that holy thoughts often abide for ever in men's memories under the form of poetry which pass away and are forgotten under the form of prose."[33]

Then, in 1854, he published three studies entitled *The Bishop, The Pastor,* and *The Preacher* in three biographical lectures. These dealt with Hugh Latimer, Richard Baxter and George Whitefield, and were to form major chapters in his later books of biography. He also began his well-known series of *Expository Thoughts on the Gospels* with the volumes on St. Matthew in 1856, on St. Mark in 1857 and on St. Luke in 1858. They were designed for use in the household pattern of prayer or the devotional reading of an average Christian family.

But the special venture of those years was the great series of tracts which were to make him known both near and far. As curate of Fawley, he had distributed tracts which he would obtain from the Religious Tract Society at Southampton;[34] now he began to write his own. His first sermon was printed and scattered broadcast as he drove about in his gig.

It was headed by a fresh and startling title: *"I have somewhat to say unto thee"* (Luke 7:40). It caught the eye, and its success led to a fresh tract in 1845. Then he tried to persuade others to join him in bringing out a series of tracts, and when no one would help he went on by himself. He had in fact entered upon one of his most fruitful activities.

Ryle had taken up the weapon forged at Oxford by the Tractarian Party and had tempered it in a new way for a new purpose. He was to write from two to three hundred tracts in all; they sold for a penny and soon had a remarkable circulation at home and in colonies overseas.[35]

In 1859 William Hunt of Ipswich published his tracts in seven small volumes with the title *Home Truths*. It was reckoned that twelve million copies of his tracts were sold in the course of his lifetime. They were widely read in foreign countries and were printed in the language of a dozen people: Welsh and Gaelic, French and German, Dutch and Danish, Spanish and Portuguese, Swedish and Norwegian, Russian and Italian, and yet others as well.[36] Crisp and pointed titles left no doubt as to their object: *Is your heart right? Have you a Priest? Are you free? Do you pray?* Plain and nervous English gave them a vogue among people of all classes on an even wider scale than that of Spurgeon's sermons. He was indeed justly designated "the prince of tract writers",[37] and his tracts proved fruitful beyond his dreams.

G.H.G. Hewitt has pointed out that in view of "the complex experience of human sin and suffering, compassion without judgement is not enough, nor is judgement without compassion".[38] Ryle's tracts had both, and the result was that letters poured in from all parts of the world to tell of their spiritual effect.

Bishop Barker in his first year in New South Wales penned a note on July 24th, 1855: "Mr. (or Mrs.) Shadforth here; converted by Ryle's tracts."[39] Mrs. Barker's unpublished diary and letters show that the Barkers always kept on hand a supply of Ryle's tracts to take with them on country journeys; she notes orders for fresh supplies and details of persons to whom they were given.[40] A Spanish translation of

*True Liberty* was read by a Dominican friar on his way to stamp out a new reform movement in Mexico. The scales fell from his eyes as he read it; he saw and grasped the truth, and went on to proclaim the faith which he had been sent to destroy.[41] Ruskin advised his friends to get any of Ryle's writings they could. "The pleasantest and most useful reading I know on nearly all religious questions whatever," he wrote, "are Ryle's tracts."[42]

"The great thing I always desired to find," Ryle had somewhat quaintly written, "was a woman who was a real Christian, who was a real lady, and who was not a fool."[43] He had been slow to marry and had fought shy of social invitations because he felt that his circumstances would not permit either course of action. He had been forced to live in an ultra frugal manner, and had often returned home to sit down and work without tea and supper.

But his position had changed for the better once he came to Helmingham and on October 29th, 1845, he married Matilda Charlotte Louisa Plumptre whose father had been converted through the ministry of Daniel Wilson and represented East Kent in the House of Commons. "I do not think marriage made any difference in my manner of living," he wrote, "and I just worked on and preached as I had done before."[44]

Their first child was born in June 1847.[45] She was baptised Georgina Matilda, the first name in memory of Georgina Tollemache who had died in July 1846 and the second name in honour of her mother. But Mrs. Ryle fell ill ten days after the birth of their daughter and at one stage little hope was held out for her recovery. She did regain her strength to some degree four months later, but she never threw off the shock to her constitution. She went to Tunbridge Wells as a convalescent until September when she was well enough to return to Helmingham. "When she got back," wrote Ryle, "I think she was happier than ever she had been before."[46] But in October she developed a cough which had its seat in her right lung, and in December on the doctor's advice, Ryle took her to Ventnor on the Isle of Wight.

It was a cold winter with mist and fog; her cough grew worse and her weakness increased. They moved in May 1848, first to Anglesey, then to Tunbridge Wells, and finally to the Plumptre home in Fredville Manor. It was to no avail; she died in June and was buried in the family vault at Norringham ten miles to the north-east from Dover.

After less than three years, Ryle found himself widowed, with a baby daughter only twelve months old; his situation was more lonely and awkward than ever. He stayed with the Plumptres for three months and then left Georgina at Fredville Manor while he returned to Helmingham. Once a month he went to Fredville Manor in order to see his daughter; he paid occasional visits to Anglesey, otherwise his work at Helmingham went on without interruption.

Then in February 1850 he married again; his new wife was Jessie Elizabeth Walker, whose father, John Walker, came from Dumfriesshire in Scotland. Their first child was born in 1851, a daughter who was named Jessie Isabelle. Three sons followed: Reginald John in 1854; Herbert Edward in 1856; and Arthur Johnston in 1857. The tenderness and affection of his homelife was in well-marked contrast with the austere figure conceived by his critics.

But, once again, his wife's ill-health placed a heavy burden on his shoulders. They had not been married more than six months before she first became very unwell; then for nearly ten years she was seldom really well for longer than three months at a time. There were long and expensive visits to London for the sake of medical attention; her health would then partially recover and they would return to Helmingham to go on much as before.

The one pleasing aspect of these enforced visits to the city was the fact that Ryle came to know all the leading Evangelical clergy and laymen in London. He was asked to preach in many parts of London; he once reckoned that he had preached in no less than sixty churches. But back in Helmingham, he was seldom able to be away from home at night in case of need; the care of children in the evenings devolved wholly on him.

Mrs. Ryle's long illness came to an end in May 1860 when she died from Bright's disease which had only been diagnosed two months before. Ryle was left more disconsolate and helpless than ever, with five children between two and fourteen years old.[47]

There is a note of self-pity in Ryle's private record of these successive bereavements which almost seems inconsistent with his general character. The same note was present in his account of his father's ruin and its chilling consequence in his own life. There are over sensitive paragraphs which he would surely have revised had he ever taken the trouble to re-write the whole story. But it was not meant for publication; its sole purpose was to tell his children the full story of God's dealings with him. He could only conclude that though all these things were against him, God meant it for good. His faith did not falter; it taught him to echo the words of the Psalmist: "As for God, His way is perfect" (Ps. 18:30).

There were other family bereavements during those years as well. In May 1846, his only brother, Frederick, died after a short illness: this had made the first gap in the Ryle family. During the fifties, his mother died and was buried beside Frederick in the churchyard at Elson in Hampshire. His youngest sister, Caroline, also died during this decade. But these losses did not touch him in the same way as the illness and death of first one wife, then the other. "Few can have any idea," so he wrote after Jessie died in 1860, "how much wear and tear and anxiety of mind and body I had to go through for at least five years."[48]

He would write from a full heart and with true understanding about Henry Venn whose wife died in 1767, leaving him with five small children. "People who have not been placed in similar circumstances may probably not understand all this," he said. "Those who have had this cross to carry can testify that there is no position in this world so trying to body and soul as that of the minister who is left a widower with a young family and a large congregation. There are anxieties in such cases which no one knows but he who has gone through them; anxieties which can crush the strongest spirit and wear out the strongest constitution."[49] It was so great a strain in his own case that he often wondered how he managed to live through it.[50]

Nor was this all. The last three years in the fifties were rendered even more painful as the result of a sharp breach between himself and John Tollemache. Nothing was so fatal to the welfare of a village community in the Victorian era as a quarrel between squire and vicar. Owen Chadwick has furnished a perfect commentary on that kind of situation in his *Victorian Miniature*.

Tollemache was an active, headstrong, impulsive, masterful man who had great physical strength and could be generous to a degree. But he was an absolute autocrat on his estate and would brook no interference. He was known as a Low Churchman who would not tolerate the growth of ritual in the livings of which he was patron. The day at the Hall always began and ended with prayers for the entire household, and no hot meals were served on Sundays.[51] He ruled his large house with a rod of iron, and he would stand up in church, watch in hand, if he thought a sermon too long.[52] Ryle once rather frightened one of the squire's daughters-in-law in much later life by telling her that the Tollemache men were very good lovers, and very good haters as well.[53]

It is not known why John Tollemache fell out with Ryle, especially during Mrs. Ryle's long illness; perhaps it was because Ryle would not put up with interruptions to his sermons; but the quarrel was so severe that all neighbourly relations came to an end.

In a sermon in March 1858, Ryle had tried to make a point about treasures on earth compared with treasures in heaven. "Will Mr. Tollemache take Peckerton Castle or Helmingham Hall or his fine house in St. James when he dies?"[54] That was too personal, and the breach was not healed even when Ryle's wife died. "This breach, I need hardly say," wrote Ryle, "as the whole parish belonged to him, made our position at Helmingham extremely uncomfortable."[55] It must have been a relief for both parties when Pelham of Norwich offered Ryle the parish of Stradbroke in 1861.

# THE VICAR OF STRADBROKE: 1861-1870

The Bishop of Norwich was John Pelham, a Christ Church man, who had been consecrated on April 30th, 1857. He was sympathetic with Evangelicals, and the offer of the living at Stradbroke to John Charles Ryle was a mark of respect which Ryle greatly valued for its own sake.

Stradbroke was only some fifteen to twenty miles away, but for Ryle it was a new world. The stipend was double that of Helmingham so that for the first time since his ordination he was financially independent. It was larger than most Suffolk villages with a population of some thirteen hundred people, four times as many as in Helmingham. There was no single dominant landlord like John Tollemache, and the vicar was by common consent the most influential person in the village.

The church was built of flint with five bays and a tower that rose like a landmark in the flat countryside.[1] It stood in the midst of farm lands which were intersected with narrow winding lanes. The people were mostly poor, and he lost no time in trying to meet their need. The church was soon packed to the doors, and few would go away disappointed.

He founded a flourishing Sunday School and supervised the erection of a village school for two hundred and fifty children. There were open-air meetings twice a week in summer and cottage meetings twice a week in winter. He once referred with half-concealed sorrow to those clergy whose main thought was for "a Nimrod, a ram-rod, or a fishing-rod":[2] they cared more for field sports such as hunting, shooting and angling than for the welfare of souls. His own concern would not even allow him to pass a group of loungers at street corners without words of admonition. "Don't stand there idle," he would say, "it would even be better if you went and got into mischief."[3] He had, in fact, embarked on the most pleasant and fruitful years of his life.

Ryle had emerged from the shadows of deep sorrow and care into a new world of sunlight and joy. This was greatly enhanced by his marriage in October 1861 to Henrietta Legh Clowes of Broughton Old Hall near Manchester. She soon proved an ideal help-mate for him and a very understanding mother for his children. They could grow up in the strong, pulsating atmosphere of a virile, manly home life in which Ryle's own robust faith was expressed with a bracing freshness.

There was nothing mawkish, nothing weakly sentimental, in his outlook; it was vividly remembered by S.R. James, afterwards the headmaster of Malvern, who had stayed in that home as a schoolboy. "Mr. Ryle," he wrote, "with his gigantic figure and stentorian voice, was perhaps rather formidable to a youthful visitor, but he was very kind and hearty. The boys, each in his own way, were delightful companions. The atmosphere of the house was devotional: daily Bible readings, somewhat lengthy family prayers, and a good deal of religious talk. But all was quite wholesome and unpretentious, and I don't think any of us were bored, much less inclined to cavil at the regime."[4]

They were never allowed to be idle; they were constantly encouraged by his disciplined indulgence. Ryle coached them at cricket, fostered their love of books, kept in touch with them at school through wise and racy letters, and followed their progress with an unflagging interest.

Herbert Ryle went up from Eton to Cambridge in 1875, and his father's feeling still shines through a letter in which he told him that no one else could ever love or care for him as much as he did.[5] And in 1876, he urged him to spend at least part of the summer with the family on holiday at Keswick. "We all like to see as much of you as we can," he wrote. " ... At our age, you can have little idea how much an old fellow like me ... counts on seeing all he can of his children."[6]

This was the man of whom Herbert Ryle was one day to write: "I, to whom it was an intense stimulus to think of pleasing my father as a boy and a young man, feel how greatly he has always filled up the picture of life."[7]

It was for the sake of his five children that in 1873 Ryle drew up a partial autobiography. This traced his life from 1816 to 1860, the year which brought the death of his second wife who was the mother of four of those children. He did not go beyond that year because he had married again in 1861 and did not wish to write about events in the lifetime of his third wife.

In 1873, Georgina was twenty-seven years old, Isabelle twenty-two, Reginald nineteen, Herbert seventeen, and Arthur sixteen. Ryle's aim was to provide them with a clear account of his conversion, his ministry, his principles, and his spiritual guide-lines for their future.[8]

There was no plan for the publication of this literary fragment; it would assuredly have been pruned and revised had he thought that it would ever appear in print. Herbert Ryle had a copy of the manuscript and this was available to Maurice Fitzgerald when he wrote his *Memoir of H.E. Ryle* in 1928.[9] He was able to quote excerpts from it in this *Memoir*, but the full text remained unknown until a copy turned up in the library of Latimer House in Oxford.

This was edited and published by Peter Toon in 1974; it was entitled *J.C. Ryle: A Self-Portrait*. It is more than doubtful whether Ryle would have cared for it to be seen by any eyes other than those of his children; it is also hard to believe that he would have liked it to be thought of as "A Self-Portrait." But it is a primary document of the utmost value for his biography and is indispensable as a source of information for the first half of his long life.

It does not deal with his work at Stradbroke although it was written in the heyday of his ministry there. But it was couched in the same clear Anglo-Saxon literary style that marked all his books and it forms a vivid commentary on the life of a country parson of strong Evangelical convictions in the early Victorian era.

All Ryle's stores of pent-up enthusiasm found release as he engaged in growing opportunities for good. His fearless sincerity, his forthright simplicity, his homely sermons, his pungent sayings, were to leave their mark in every corner of the parish; his name was still a force to be reckoned with in Stradbroke fifty years after his sojourn there had come to an end.[10]

This feeling was reciprocal, for in 1886 at the Wakefield Church Congress, he recalled the years he had spent there with a sense of nostalgic affection. He spoke of the village "with its grand Gothic church, and its little cluster of cottages round it, and its two or three humble shops, with its total absence of urban temptations, with its few hundreds of people within easy walking of the parsonage, with seats in the church for almost every inhabitant and places in the school for almost every child".[11]

People looked up to him as one who was "every inch a man. His tall robust frame was matched with a strength of purpose and a directness of speech which was eminently bracing. No one could doubt he was one whose religion was intensely real."[12]

There was more than enough to do in his own parish, but he was in great demand for pulpit or platform all over the country. The two nearest railway stations for Stradbroke were Diss and Harleston. Each was eight or nine miles away, and he often had to drive to one or other of them. Often enough it was a race with time, and Ryle used to call out through the carriage window: "Garnham, we shall lose the train." The coachman's reply was always the same: "I can't go faster, Sir, unless the horses gallop." And Ryle would shout again as only he could shout: "Then make them gallop." And the horses would dash through the main street of Harleston at a pace that brought people running to their doors to see "old Ryle late again".[13]

During the years 1859-60 England had been deeply

stirred by a movement which has been called the second Evangelical awakening. In the aftermath of that Revival during 1861, Suffolk received a visit from two Evangelists. One was Reginald Radcliffe, a well-known solicitor from Liverpool; the other was Thomas Shouldham Henry, the son of the President of Queen's College, Belfast. Ryle had acted as one of their sponsors when they came to Ipswich; then in June they came to Stradbroke where they held open-air meetings on the village green and other special meetings in the Corn Hall.[14]

It was a great start for his new life at Stradbroke where his own work was to centre on preaching. But he did not confine himself to the pulpit; he was convinced that evangelism and education ought to go hand in hand. This was why he addressed himself from the outset to the need for a school which would provide for all children in the parish.

He was largely responsible for the building of such a school at a cost of thirteen hundred pounds which was mostly found from local benefactors. The school was ready for use in 1864 and was linked with the National School Society whose task was to co-ordinate the work of such parish schools throughout the country. One classroom was reserved for the conduct of a private school for the sons of farmers and tradesmen, and the playground was divided by a fence in order to separate them from other children. "Middle class people would not have sent their children to school with those whom they considered to be the riff raff of society."[15]

Ryle took such things as he found them; his great concern was to provide for the education of rich and poor alike, for he thought of education as a handmaid of the Gospel. He looked upon religious instruction in the school as an essential part of his ministry, and he drew on the help of his wife as well as his curates to ensure that this task was adequately performed.

Ryle had seven curates in all while he was at Stradbroke, and they eased the burden of work in the parish. Social welfare activities in the modern sense were hardly visualised, but he did his best to keep up the tone of the village. He thought that rich and poor would always be found side by side; it was not his task to try to resolve social problems.

When the social movement came to Suffolk through the newly founded Agricultural Labourers Union, Ryle was little inclined to hold out the hand of welcome. Joseph Arch, who was its leader, was a Primitive Methodist lay preacher and was motivated by serious Christian principles. But Ryle believed that a minister of the Gospel should not interfere in such matters. Had not Jesus said: "Man, who made me a judge or a divider over you?" (Luke 12:14). The new movement did not disturb the peace of his parish; it could only muster a few members, unlike other parts of Suffolk.[16]

His point of view was set out in forthright language at the Croydon Church Congress in 1877.

If the country clergyman will only live the life he ought to live and preach as he ought to preach, he will find as good friends amongst the poor as in any class in the land. I have no fear whatever for the Church of England in rural districts if the clergy are only faithful to their ordination vows and to the Word of God. The poor are not such bad judges as some people think and in the long run I believe they will not think the Chapel better than the Church if the clergy only do their duty. But in the matter of the Unions, my sentence is that the clergy had better not interfere with them. Let them mind their own business and remember that business is to live and preach the Gospel.[17]

Peter Toon's comment on this statement is apposite. "Herein," he wrote, "lay both the strength and the weakness of Ryle":[18] great strength in his commitment to evangelism; weakness in his lack of understanding for a major social development.

It was while in Suffolk that his reading of the masters of

the English Reformation and his favourite Puritan authors put their mettle into his soul. He could make time in a country parish as few city clergy could do to soak his mind in the works of the great divines and he hammered out his theology on the anvil of wide and hard reading.

He could describe himself as a moderate Calvinist, a follower of Amyraldus rather than of Toplady, one who would not limit the death of Christ in the application of its saving value but would freely invite all men to draw near in humble, reverent believing. He soon became known far beyond Suffolk as an earnest preacher of the old school and he received invitations which were to take him all over England.

H.C.G. Moule was to recall how in 1856 he had listened as a boy to sermons preached by Ryle as well as others to large and attentive congregations.[19] Henry Venn was present at a clerical conference held at Weston-Super-Mare in 1858 when "Ryle preached a noble sermon... which was listened to with deep attention for an hour and a half".[20] F.J. Chavasse at Oxford in 1866 "listened to such masters as Pusey, Goulburn, Liddon, Trench and J.C. Ryle".[21]

He was at his best in exposition of the leading doctrines of the Gospel, and such preaching always came from the heart. "I would go to the stake, God helping me," he once declared, "for the glorious truth that in the matter of justification before God, every believer is complete in Christ."[22] This was the great touchstone of his experience, and he applied it as strongly as he could in all his preaching. "Faith is the only thing required in order that you and I may be forgiven," so he declared. "That we will come by faith to Jesus as sinners with our sins... and forsaking all other hope, cleave only to Him, this is all and everything that God asks for. Let a man only do this, and he shall be saved... His sins are clean gone, and his soul is justified in God's sight, however bad and guilty he may have been."[23]

Ryle brought the same skill to bear in biography and two volumes were published in 1868 in order to revive popular interest in the makers of true Evangelical continuity. They had grown out of *The Bishop, The Pastor,* and *The Preacher* which had appeared in 1854.

The first bore the title *Bishops and Clergy of Other Days*; it had chapters on five leading figures in the sixteenth and seventeenth centuries. Other chapters were written in later years and in its final form it was called *Light From Old Times.* In the Introduction to the 1890 edition, Ryle made a bold claim for the martyrs of the English Reformation. "None were so often talked of round English firesides," he wrote. "... None... so thoroughly deserve to be had in honour. They were men of whom the Church of England may well be proud. She may reckon among her sons some perhaps who were their equals; but none, I am sure, who were their superiors."[24]

This volume was followed in the same year by *Christian Leaders in the Last Century*, and this book dealt with the fathers of the Evangelical Revival. They were all there: Whitefield, Wesley, Romaine, Berridge, Henry Venn and Grimshaw as well as some who are still less well known. It was not a critical history, but was written with a racy mixture of personal narrative and judicious anecdote which gave it an exciting quality. "I believe firmly," he declared, "that... the world has seen no such men since the days of the apostles. I believe there have been none who have preached so much clear Scriptural truth, none who have lived such lives, none who have shown such courage in Christ's service, none who have suffered so much for the truth, none who have done so much good. If any one can name better men, he knows more than I do."[25]

It was during these years that the Oxford Movement lost its original Tractarian flavour and passed into the hands of the Ritualists. Ryle had never ceased to deplore the strong bias of this Movement against the whole ethos of the Protestant character of the Church of England, and he thought that it was arrant nonsense to talk as though the Church held a kind of middle status between Dissent and Rome. "We might as well talk of the Isle of Wight being mid-way between England and France."[26]

Two of the most trenchant pamphlets which he ever wrote were trumpet calls for churchmen to weigh their debt to the Reformation,[27] and he pronounced his own verdict in the ringing oratory of the Victorian era: "There is a voice in the blood of the martyrs. What does that voice say? It cries aloud from Oxford, Smithfield and Gloucester. Resist to the death the Popish doctrine of the Real Presence under the forms of the consecrated bread and wine in the Lord's Supper!"[28]

He had too much independent courage to hold his peace when he saw that vital doctrines for which English martyrs had died were once more in danger, and his outspoken reaction could not fail to provoke strong dislike in many quarters. "When I go down to the valley of the shadow of death," he wrote, "and my feet touch the cold waters, I want something better than vague high-sounding words or the painted play-things and gilded trifles of man-made ceremonial. Give me no stone altars and would-be confessors. Give me no surpliced priests or pretended sacrifice in my bedroom. Put no man or form between me and Christ."[29]

He would always allow that the Church is largely comprehensive, but he argued that its limits had been defined by the Thirty-Nine Articles and the Book of Common Prayer: and he hit out with all his strength against things outside those limits which threatened to destroy the true Protestant tradition of the Church of England. This was why a contemporary article said that he was "all round the particular, the exceptional, the absolute aversion of the High Churchman".[30]

E.L. Woodward in *The Age of Reform* points out that the Evangelicals had one thing to impress on the world of their time: that was the need for the renewal of true religion both in heart and in home. Their continued insistence on personal holiness was to transform the old Low Church party which had represented the most arid type of religious whiggery. But their weakness had been their long neglect of history and theology; they had clung too firmly to a narrow literalism in their interpretation of the received text of Scripture. They strove to save men's souls, but the younger generation began to drift away from a society which was afraid of new ideas.[31]

It was into this void that a group of scholars dropped a bombshell in the form of Essays and Reviews in 1860. This was a claim for the right to maintain "new and dangerous opinions within the pale of the Church of England",[32] and it was as bold an experiment in an opposite direction as Tract XC had been twenty years before. It was treated as a wanton attack on the inspiration of the Bible, and the Tractarians under Pusey were as little prepared to meet it as the Evangelicals under Lord Shaftesbury.

The atmosphere was explosive, and men like Ryle had to declare themselves under the strong glare of controversy. He did not hesitate. "Let us regard all who would damage the authority of the Bible, or impugn its credit, as spiritual robbers," he said. "... What do they offer as a safer guide and better provision for our souls? Nothing. Absolutely nothing... substantial and real."[33]

He lived to see English scholars take their cue from German critics in the literary analysis of the Bible, and it fell to younger men to meet them on the ground of textual criticism. His own response marks both the strength and the weakness of his school of thought in the first stages of this conflict. "I feel no hesitation," he wrote, "in avowing that I believe in the plenary inspiration of every word of the original text of Holy Scripture."[34] He held to this view with all its difficulties, and was content to wait until time should resolve the doubts; but while he had to wait, his faith stood like a rock.

When this storm was at its height in 1862, Ryle preached the annual sermon for the Church Missionary Society on the subject of St. Paul at Athens. The whole address was summed up in its three crisp points: what St. Paul saw; what St. Paul felt; what St. Paul did (Acts 17:16-17).

It drove home the fact of man's need for a divine revelation of truth by a vivid picture of the idolatry which filled the most cultured city in the old world. "So long as the Bible is the Bible," he said, "... it is a solemn duty to feel for the souls of the heathen... Compassion we ought to feel when we think of the wretched state of unconverted souls... No poverty like this poverty! No disease like this disease! No slavery like this slavery! No death like this death in idolatry, irreligion, and sin!"[35] Eugene Stock furnished a comment on the effect of this sermon. "It is needless to say," he wrote, "how easy the application was to the broad views that were becoming fashionable."[36]

In May 1864, Ryle was on the platform at the Society's annual meeting shortly before Samuel Crowther's consecration as the Bishop of the Niger Ryle spoke of the early missionaries who had gone out to the white man's grave at Sierra Leone, bearing the seed which had at last brought forth its sheaves. Then, pointing to Crowther on the platform, he threw out a challenge to the Broad Church school to produce one sheaf like him.[37]

He preached before the Church Pastoral Aid Society both in 1868 and in 1882, and the latter sermon was a severe castigation of those who try to keep a foot in all camps while their soul belongs to none. They "think it a mark of cleverness and intellect to have no decided opinions about anything in religion," he said, "and to be utterly unable to make up their minds as to what is Christian truth... They think everybody is right and nobody wrong, everything is true and nothing is false, all sermons are good and none are bad... They are... ever ready for new things because they have no firm grasp on the old."[38] Such words were blunt enough and not without harshness, but he would not budge from his strong faith in the Word of God. "Here is rock," he wrote, "all else is sand."[39]

The growth of Ritualism on the one hand and of Modernism on the other were the forces that led to the formation of the London Church Association in 1865. Ryle had become increasingly involved in the issue to which Evangelicals had to address themselves in the Church as a whole. He hoped that the London Church Association would become the basis of a wider union of all Evangelical churchmen.

In an address at the Islington Clerical Conference in January 1868, he spoke of the dangers which loomed ahead for the Church of England. This address was published as a pamphlet and was widely distributed. It was written in his style of trenchant vigour and it bore the title, *We Must Unite*. He asked:

Is there a want of organised union among Evangelical churchmen? I answer that question without hesitation in the affirmative. In the main we preach the same doctrines and hold the same opinions. In the main we support the same societies, go to the same meetings, subscribe to the same charities, work our parishes in the same way, go to the same booksellers' shops, read the same books, papers and magazines, and groan and sigh over the same evils in the world. But there our union stops. For defending common principles, for resisting common enemies, for facing common dangers, for attaining common great objects, for harmonious conduct in circumstances of great perplexity, for decided, prompt, energetic action in great emergencies, for all this I say unhesitatingly, we have no organised union at all. Every Evangelical churchman does what is right in his own eyes and every district goes to work in its own way. We have God's truth on our side. We have numbers, strength, goodwill and desires to do what is right; but from lack of organisation, we are weak as water.[40]

But Ryle's vision for a strong, united Evangelical Association was never realised; unity among Evangelicals was a matter of spiritual affinity rather than of organised cohesion.

A new development in church activities was marked by the first Church Congress which was held in 1861. Speakers from all parties were made welcome on the Congress platform, and the Ritualists were quick to seize the chance to put forward their most extravagant ideas. Representative Evangelicals were slow to come forward: they fought shy of sitting side by side with men whose views filled them with mistrust.

Ryle took his place on the Congress platform for the first time in 1866 when he did so at the request of the Bishop of Norwich in whose see city the Congress was held that year. He was convinced by that experience that non-attendance was a mistake and he was an active participant in the years that followed.

He was far ahead of his more cautious Evangelical contemporaries in boldness and vision, and he argued that it would be wrong to concede the whole movement to one restless revolutionary faction within the Church.[41] He urged it as a plain duty for men of his school to attend, and he was soon joined by Edward Hoare and Edward Garbett. It was not so easy to draw others from his party, but he refused to let the chance slip by default.

He brought the whole question before the Church Association in 1869 and again before the Islington Clerical Conference in 1872. He was hotly opposed in some quarters and was denounced in one paper as a Neo-Evangelical.[42] But he carried the day, and after the sixties, there was always a fair muster of Evangelicals at Congress meetings.

Criticism broke out from time to time, and in 1878 he wrote a tract with the pointed title, *Shall We Go?* The Church at large was no longer allowed to say that the Evangelical school of thought was of no account. "I believe," he wrote, "some High Churchmen and Broad Churchmen have discovered for the first time that Evangelical Churchmen read and think, and are not always unlearned and ignorant men. They have discovered that they love the Church of England from their standpoint as much as any, and that they are not dissenting wolves in sheep's clothing. They have discovered not least that they can talk courteously and considerately, and that they are not at all unmannerly, rude, Johnsonian bears."[43]

The Church Congress, *par seul*, had no magnetic

attraction for Ryle, but he felt a frank exchange of views on a neutral platform would at least help churchmen to a better understanding of each other.[44] "I have always held," he wrote, "that truth is most likely to be reached when men on all sides conceal nothing, but tell out all their minds."[45]

He was himself a master of debate; courteous, incisive, resourceful, never afraid to speak his mind. He won equal recognition as a resolute advocate of what he believed to be right, and a determined opponent of what he believed to be wrong. It might not be hard to find fault with things that were said on the spur of the moment, but his own good humour and his complete freedom from all personal invective were great assets on the platform.

The Dean of Cork, W.C. Magee, afterwards Archbishop of York, had observed in 1865 that a Prayer Book in the style of Tractarians like Skinner and Bennett would be deplorable, but that he had no wish to see a Prayer Book in the style of men like Ryle and Close.[46] But after the Congress at Dublin in 1868, he spoke in the warmest terms of "the frank and manly Mr. Ryle."[47]

Eugene Stock considered that it was at Southampton in 1870 that Ryle clinched his reputation. The most interesting debate was on reunion, and Ryle made a bold plea for church reform as an immediate pre-requisite: "Repeal the Act of Uniformity! Shorten the Services! Use the Laity!" The great audience found it contagious, and each fresh point evoked rounds of applause. When he ventured to think that the Church would have fared better had John Wesley become Archbishop of Canterbury, he was cheered with amazing enthusiasm. But when he urged men to join the Bible Society, there was a cry of "No!" He at once said that the Non-Conformists had just been asked to share in the preparation of a Revised Version of the Bible. "If we may unite to revise our Bible," he cried, "why not also to print and circulate it?" The riposte was complete, and the cheering broke out again after one of the best speeches ever heard at a Church Congress.[48]

Ryle's star had certainly been in the ascendant throughout the sixties although it had yet to reach its zenith. He had become the most trusted of all contemporary Evangelical clergy and was perhaps the first undisputed leader in their ranks since the days of John Newton and Charles Simeon.

He had spent his early life in Cheshire, and he liked to say that "no county breeds better and taller men".[49] He was himself a man of fine bearing and great natural dignity. He stood six feet two in his shoes, so he told a Bootle tea party in 1897, and a full beard added to his impressive appearance.[50] His tall figure and good looks gave him an almost regal presence; his strong voice and genial character were marks of one who was born to command.

Such gifts were matched by a virility of thought and an independence of speech which were eminently bracing. He stood head and shoulders above the rank and file in true spiritual stature; he was second to none either in breadth of vision or strength of purpose. Nothing could shake his faith in the saving virtue of the Gospel, and this helped to invigorate his words with a sturdy optimism. "Has Evangelical religion any distinctive principles?" he asked. "I answer it has. Are they worth contending for? I answer, they are."[51]

He read the signs of the times with cool and clear-eyed judgement, and none saw more clearly the dark waters into which the Church was drifting. His grave warnings never made light of the peril, but he refused to give up hope. His words from the platform had a rugged appeal which men could not mistake: "No surrender! No desertion! No compromise! No disgraceful peace!"[52] There was at least no doubt that when Ryle spoke, men would hear the ringing tones of absolute clarity. He liked to quote St. Paul's famous dictum and to order his own conduct accordingly: "If the trumpet give an uncertain sound, who shall prepare himself to the battle?" (1 Cor. 14:8).

# THE VICAR OF STRADBROKE: 1871-1880

Ryle's main project within the parish during the seventies
was a major undertaking in order to restructure the interior
of the church at Stradbroke. This had become necessary as
a result of the growing numbers in the congregation; there
were people who used to travel as much as twenty miles in
order to hear him preach.

He made his first appeal for help in a letter which he sent
out in December 1870.

> After standing probably four hundred and fifty years,
> almost every part of this noble fabric requires more or
> less repair and renovation.... It is quite impossible for
> the inhabitants of Stradbroke to raise such a sum as two
> thousand seven hundred pounds... There are no resident
> landlords or gentry and the population is made up of
> farmers, labourers, tradesmen and three professional
> men... I make bold to express a hope that many
> unknown friends in Great Britain and Ireland who have
> for 20 years read and approved the writings of the Vicar
> of Stradbroke will now kindly remember the church in
> which he preaches and generously aid him in the heavy
> work he has undertaken.[1]

The old box pews were replaced; a new organ and choir
stalls were provided; the old Jacobean pulpit was removed
and a new pulpit took its place. On April 3rd, 1872, the
Bishop of Norwich came to Stradbroke to preach at a

special service to mark the reopening of the church after the work on its restoration was complete.[2]

Nor was that all. Ryle spent five hundred pounds out of his own pocket on a new roof; but he was in need of another five hundred to complete further work on the chancel. He made a fresh appeal in December 1878. "Time is short and life uncertain," he wrote. "Before the connection of the present Vicar of Stradbroke with his parish is ended, he is anxious to leave... his church a complete pattern of what the house of God ought to be in the Reformed Church of England."[3] The church building did not come first in Ryle's way of thinking: nothing could displace the priority which belonged to the proclamation of the Gospel. But he did all that he could to make the church a home for worship in an atmosphere of reverence and dignity.

Recognition of Ryle came from many quarters during these years and his growing reputation made him a man to mark and watch. He had become rural dean of Hoxne in 1870; this gave him a certain degree of pastoral oversight for twenty-five parishes whose centre was Stradbroke. Bishop Pelham required rural deans to hold two meetings for the clergy each year and to submit yearly reports on each parish.[4]

Then in 1872 Pelham made him an honorary canon of Norwich so that he became an occasional preacher in the cathedral. He took an active part in the movement to establish an annual Diocesan Conference, and in 1871 he published a paper which he had read to the Home Counties Clerical and Lay Association. It was entitled *A Churchman's Duty about Diocesan Conferences*, and it urged his brethren to come forward and to labour incessantly to make them what they ought to be. He was equally in favour of a "collective Conference" at which each parish would be represented.

The first Conference for the Diocese of Norwich was held in 1872, but Ryle was ill and could neither attend nor speak. The next Conference for Norwich was in 1879 and was on an elective basis with representatives for each rural deanery.[5]

Ryle had also spoken regularly at the Islington Clerical Conference since 1860 and at the Church Association since 1865. He maintained both interests in the seventies and continued to appear on the platform of the Church Congress: at Nottingham and Leeds in 1871 and 1872; at Brighton and Croydon in 1874 and 1877; at Sheffield and Swansea in 1878 and 1879; and at Leicester in 1880.

He was Select Preacher for the University of Cambridge in 1873 and 1874, and for the University of Oxford in 1874, 1875, 1876, 1879 and 1880. He was also closely involved in the foundation of Wycliffe Hall at Oxford in 1877 and of Ridley Hall at Cambridge in 1879. A man of mark indeed.

Strenuous endeavours for church reform were fostered by the Ritualists throughout the seventies, and their efforts caused a vigorous reaction among churchmen with a conservative outlook. But no one could suspect Ryle of trimming, and his views on the need for church reform, although of an opposite character to those of the Ritualists, were almost as revolutionary.

The church courts and canon law were under constant debate, and he had shrewd comments to make on the situation which had evolved. He spoke strongly against those who decried the great lawsuits which had taken place in order to secure a verdict on the validity of the innovations for which Ritualists had been responsible, for he believed that the judgements of the Privy Council had saved the Church from the verge of ruin.[6] "No doubt," he wrote, "the present Court of Final Appeal, like every judicial court composed of men, may have its faults and imperfections, and the Royal Commission on Ecclesiastical Courts may possibly have suggested some improvements; but if the Judicial Committee of the Privy Council is to be set aside in ecclesiastical cases and so called spiritual court set up in its stead, I doubt extremely whether a better court, and one which will satisfy the laity, can possibly be constructed."[7]

He would never assent to plans which sought to sweep away the old Court of Appeal in order to create a new Court of Bishops only; but he thought that canon law could well be reformed in a way that would clear up most of the problems.

He was surprisingly modern in this respect, for he argued that the canons should be revised so as to give the Church a new charter. "We want," he wrote, "a new set of canons for the regulation of all the proceedings of the Church of England. Those that we have at present are many of them practically useless, and little more than fossils, rendered needless by alterations of law."[8] But he could not foresee how this would be turned to account with quite another emphasis after two great world wars.

A still more vexed question was the plan to restore a more active role to Convocation which ever since 1717 had met only to present an address to the Crown and then to suffer itself to be prorogued.

It was believed by the leaders of the Oxford Movement that if Convocation could be revived as a legislative unit, they would secure a church body which would reverse the Gorham judgement of 1850. This had emanated from the Judicial Committee of the Privy Council and had confirmed Evangelicals in their rejection of the doctrine of baptismal regeneration. Evangelicals had no wish to risk their future with a revitalised Convocation, and such a threat drove them into active opposition.

But Ryle was far ahead of most of his brethren on this subject, just as he had been in the case of the Congress movement. He was convinced that the powers of Convocation would be revived, whether they liked or not, and he wanted to place his own plan for reform first in the field. He was able to state his views at the Congress at Leeds in 1872 and he bluntly declared that Convocation should be mended rather than ended: that Canterbury and York should unite in a single province; that there should be fewer *ex officio* and more elected members; and that laymen should be represented.[9]

Few could combine common sense and candid speech more effectively than Ryle, but these outspoken proposals were too bold at a time when so many people were still vaguely afraid of change. He held to his course in spite of Ritualist innovations on one side and conservative timidity on the other because he was convinced that such a course was true to the basic ideals of the Church of England. He wrote:

Once for all, I protest against the charge that I am no true churchman because I hold the opinions that I do. In the matter of true and real attachment to the Church of England, I will not give place by subjection to those who are called High Churchmen for one moment. Have they signed the Thirty-Nine Articles *ex animo* and *bona fide*? So have I. Have they declared their full assent to the Liturgy and all things contained in it? So have I. Do they honour the Sacraments? So do I. Do they think them generally necessary to salvation? So do I. Do they labour for the prosperity of the Church? So do I.[10]

Ryle cherished a lifelong concern for evangelism and was never more at home than in the proclamation of the everlasting Gospel. His own preaching was that of a moderate Calvinist, but that did not detract from the honour in which he held such men as John Wesley and Fletcher of Madeley.

For his own part, he made a remarkable statement in 1887. "It is only thirty years ago," he said, "that I had the high honour of taking part in the first mission service which, I believe, was ever held. It was for six evenings successively in St. Martin's Church, Birmingham, and Dr. McNeile, Dr. Miller, and myself were the preachers."[11] It was thought a very dubious experiment at the time, but parish missions were to become acceptable features of church life during the next thirty years.

Ryle had sponsored the visit of Radcliffe to Ipswich and Stradbroke in 1861; twelve years later, he gave his wholehearted support to Moody and Sankey in their missions throughout England. They had arrived at Liverpool in the summer of 1872, but two men less likely to set England on fire could hardly be imagined. They made their way first to Scotland, then to Ireland, and it became clear in no time that the unknown Moody was the greatest Evangelist since George Whitefield. Unlike Whitefield, his voice was harsh; he spoke with a nasal accent; there was nothing theatrical; even Sankey's solos were no more than simple hymns which he played on a small harmonium. But the largest buildings could not hold the crowds that came to hear him, and hundreds of people remained behind as inquirers.

They returned to England late in 1874 and their visit reached its culminating point in the great London mission of 1875. Herbert Ryle, who was at Eton, was not impressed; he wrote a rather cynical letter to his step-mother in June: "I do not know that I was very much struck by either 'Soody' or 'Mankey'. 'Soody' preached not much different from what father would have done, except with slightly more coarseness, without heads and with rather longer stories and illustrations."[12] But Ryle welcomed Moody with all his heart; he rejoiced in preaching that was thoroughly biblical, eminently sane and level-headed, and so amazingly effective in the enduring conversion of young and old.

Ryle's support for Moody was in total contrast with his opposition to the movement which had sprung up at much the same time to promote personal holiness. William Pennefather had organised the Mildmay Conference each year since 1856 in order to encourage growth in holy living.

Among the speakers were such men as the Bonars from Scotland, Lord Radstock and Reginald Radcliffe, and there were no novel views of Christian perfection. But in 1870, an American Quaker named Robert Pearsall Smith published a little book called *Holiness Through Faith* and in 1872 he and his wife came to England where they were soon caught up in a round of meetings.

In July 1874, a Convention was held in the beautiful grounds of Broadlands; this led to a further Convention at

Oxford in September "for the promotion of Scriptural holiness."[13] Ryle had been in general agreement with a critical review of Pearsall Smith's book by G.T. Fox of Durham and he watched the growing popularity of the Pearsall Smiths with concern. He thought that their teaching tended towards Christian perfection and he helped to convene a Conference in February 1875 for a careful study of the Scriptural position. He was too ill at the time to attend, and the next move took place when the Brighton Convention was held in June that year. It was attended by more than six thousand people, but the critics were far from reassured.

Ryle joined those who wrote to *The Record* to voice his grave concern, saying that the difference between Moody's teaching and that of the Pearsall Smiths was "the difference between sunshine and fog".[14] This was borne out by the sudden collapse of Pearsall Smith who had to return to America. He lacked both mental and moral stability, and his failure seemed to highlight the worst fears of Ryle and other critics. They were genuinely afraid that the new teaching on holiness by faith would lead to an untenable doctrine of sinless perfection.

It was in these circumstances that the first Convention was held at Keswick in July 1875. It was convened by Canon Harford Battersby on a semi-private basis and with little idea that it would grow into an annual Convention which would attract thousands and would touch the ends of the earth. But misgiving was still persistent in many quarters and Ryle's sentiments had not diminished. "Ryle," wrote John Kent, "was a man of certainties, belonging to the generation of whom F.D. Maurice said that in all their attitudes, they started from sin and not from God."[15]

Ryle's great primary objection to the holiness movement was his belief that it was seriously defective in its teaching on sin. This was clearly set out in a book which he wrote as an answer to the views which he thought were so unsound. This book was called *Holiness* and was published in 1877. It was enlarged and re-issued in 1879.

The first chapter was starkly headed "Sin", and the first page declared that "the plain truth is that a right knowledge of sin lies at the root of all saving Christianity".[16] Pearsall Smith had claimed in *Holiness Through Faith* that we may be cleansed not only from the stain of sin, but from sin itself. Ryle would have none of that. "I must protest," he wrote, "against the language used in many quarters . . . about perfection."[17]

Pearsall Smith was on surer ground when he argued that we ought not to expect defeat in the pursuit of holiness. But that was not enough for Ryle. He knew that there must be conflict as well as faith in the struggle to overcome, and that conflict would be unreal if defeat were impossible. Pearsall Smith's teaching was "a by-product of an American world suffering from the strains on American society which were produced but were not healed by the Civil War".[18] Ryle was acute enough to recognise this element in *Holiness Through Faith* teaching, and he would not accept what he could not prove from Holy Scripture.

Ryle went as far as he could in recognition of the aims of Keswick leaders and tried to write with courtesy and charity.

> Do they think that a higher standard of Christian living is needed in the present day? So do I. Do they think that clearer, stronger, fuller teaching about holiness is needed? So do I. Do they think that Christ ought to be more exalted as the root and author of sanctification as well as justification? So do I. Do they think that believers should be urged more and more to live by faith? So do I. Do they think that a very close walk with God should be more pressed on believers as the secret of happiness and usefulness? So do I. In all these things we agree. But if they want to go further, then I ask them to take care where they tread.[19]

That was in 1877; in 1879, he went further: "Towards those who think holiness is to be promoted by the modern, so-called spiritual life movement, I feel nothing but charity. If they do good, I am thankful. Towards myself and those who agree with me, I ask them to feel charity in return."[20]

The spectre of Pearsall Smith's teaching had begun to fade. Ryle preached in the parish church in Keswick on the Sunday before the 1879 Convention, but did not stay for the week-day meetings: he went as far as he could from friendship and respect for Harford-Battersby, but no further.

Yet that was not quite all. Ryle's younger friend, H.C.G. Moule of Ridley Hall in Cambridge, shared his misgivings in the light of a conversation with Pearsall Smith in 1874. Ten years later, Moule wrote a series of four articles for *The Record* entitled "Holiness". They were a careful review of a book by Evan Hopkins called *The Law of Liberty in the Spiritual Life*, and they mingled sincere respect for the author with stringent criticism of his teaching. But some three months later, Moule went through an experience which swept his doubts aside and in July 1886 he made his first appearance on the Keswick platform. Moule soon became the real theologian of the movement, a fact that was not lost on Ryle. His mood was to soften, though he could not dismiss all his reservations. He would neither appear on the platform, nor go to the meetings.

Ryle was a man of untiring industry in the cure of souls: his voice was never silent; his pen was never idle. The two great marks of his preaching were simplicity and sincerity, and the result was a style of great strength in its clear and forceful address. His work as a country vicar brought him into touch with humble hearers who had no use for the literary finesse or the polished oratory of a Liddon or a Farrar. His one great aim was to speak to their hearts in a way that would make them weigh the things of time on the scales of eternity.

His views on the subject of simplicity in preaching were most fully expressed in a paper prepared for the Homiletical Society and read at St. Paul's Cathedral in 1882.[21] He made it clear that this was an art which he had been forced to learn through sheer necessity. "I deliberately say," he declared, "that I would rather preach before the University at Oxford or Cambridge, or the Temple, or Lincoln's Inn, or the Houses of Parliament, than I would address an agricultural congregation on a fine hot afternoon in the month of August."[22]

The whole paper is, in fact, a full-length portrait of Ryle himself as a preacher. He kept before his mind the need to have a firm grasp of the text, to use plain words in a lucid composition, to speak direct to the heart and conscience, and to employ apt and homely illustrations. He thought that the finest models of plain modern English were John Bright and William Cobbett. "The best English writer for the last hundred years," he said, "was William Cobbett ... I think he wrote the finest simple Saxon-English the world has ever seen."[23] And he admired both Bunyan and Spurgeon for their command of a pointed Anglo-Saxon style and diction, used with common sense and telling effect.

His own style was comparable in its robust simplicity, and it achieved one main purpose: he kept rustic farm-hands awake on a mid-summer afternoon, and they could not mistake his meaning or purpose.

There is no doubt that Ryle's dignified mastery of a plain style gave his words a thrust and drive of great power. He was always terse and fresh and adept in the art of coining vigorous epigrams which were easily remembered. There are numerous examples: "What we weave in time we wear in eternity"; "It is hard for an empty bag to stand upright"; "Meddle with no man's person, but spare no man's sin."[24]

It was his great desire to point man in his guilt to the God of all grace and to "blow the trumpet of the everlasting Gospel loud and long".[25] It was in full accord with this desire that when a new pulpit was placed in the church at Stradbroke, he had a text carved round its top so that his eye could not fail to catch sight of its emphatic injunction. The text was his watchword as a preacher, as it had been St. Paul's: "Woe is unto me, if I preach not the Gospel" (1 Cor.

9:16). He stood by and looked on while the workmen carved the letters; then he took the chisel into his own hands and cut a deep groove beneath the one word "not".[26] It is interesting to know that a deeply scored line beneath that word may still be seen.

The style of the spoken sermon still rings through the printed format: one passage may suffice as an illustration of his appeal to the conscience.

That grand old bell in St. Paul's Cathedral, London, which has struck the hours for so many years is seldom heard by many during the business hours of the day. The roar and din of traffic in the streets have a strange power to deaden its sound and prevent men hearing it. But when the daily work is over, and desks are locked, and doors are closed, and books are put away, and quiet reigns in the great city, the case is altered. As the old bell at night strikes eleven, and twelve, and one, and two, and three, thousands hear it who never heard it during the day. And so I hope it will be with many an one in the matter of his soul. Now in the plenitude of health and strength, in the hurry and whirl of business, I fear the voice of your conscience is often stifled and you cannot hear it. But the day may come when the great bell of conscience will make itself heard, whether you like it or not.[27]

Ryle's first major literary work to be published during those years marked the completion of his *Expository Thoughts on The Gospels.* He had brought out single volumes on the Gospels of St. Matthew and St. Mark in 1856 and 1857; then came two more volumes on the Gospel of St. Luke in 1858 and 1859.

He had embarked on this series with a purely devotional object in view: the books were meant for daily use in the home as expositions which could be read aloud when the family assembled for prayers. This was explained in the preface to the volume on St. Matthew's Gospel. "I have tried to place myself," he wrote, "in the position of one who is reading aloud to others and must arrest their attention if he can."[28]

But this plan was greatly enlarged when he came to deal with St. John's Gospel and his first ten or twelve years at Stradbroke saw the steady development of a much more ample commentary. He retained his pattern for the devotional exposition of each passage, but he added a new feature for those who longed for a deeper knowledge of the Gospel. The devotional sections were supplemented with notes on each verse in small print packed with useful material.

In 1873, the finished work was published in three volumes which were to win widespread recognition as a valuable contribution in the field of New Testament studies. Their real merit must be judged in view of the fact that they were written before the rise of the Cambridge school of scientific exegesis under Lightfoot, Westcott and Hort. Ryle's notes quote from at least eighty authors with a remarkable eye for detail. He had combed the fathers and schoolmen, reformers and puritans, with an equal zest for information. He assessed their value and then frankly declared: "Happy would it be for the Church of England if all her clergy knew their Bibles as well as such men as Ferus and Toletus."[29]

One of the most helpful features of this commentary was the fact that while he observed what other men believed, he went on to declare what he himself believed and to state the ground on which that belief was formed. He would leave no room for doubt if he could help it.

Ryle wrote just as he preached, and his books have the same homely vigour as his sermons. The flow of books, tracts and pamphlets went on without ceasing, and their circulation was to touch the ends of the earth. They were treasured in the homes of Tasmanian farmers, as for example at Aul Derrig, Northdown, as much as his sermons were in Stradbroke.

The most influential volume which he published during

the seventies was *Knots Untied*: it first saw the light of day in 1874, but was to be constantly re-issued during the next one hundred years. Ryle stated his purpose in the preface with his customary directness and clarity: "It consists of nineteen papers on subjects which are matters of dispute among English Churchmen in the present day, systematically arranged. A moment's glance at the table of contents will show that there is hardly any point of theological controversy belonging to this era which is not discussed with more or less fulness in these papers."[30]

The first chapter dealt with Evangelical religion, what it is and what it is not, and set the tone for all that followed. "By Evangelical Religion", he wrote, "I do not mean Christianity as compared with Heathenism, or Protestantism as compared with Romanism, or Trinitarianism as compared with Socinianism."[31] He meant that view of truth whose distinctive principles are found in Holy Scripture, in the Thirty-Nine Articles, in the Book of Common Prayer, in the works of the reformers and in the writings of the pre-Caroline divines.

He knew that his opinions were not popular in the Church as a whole, but they were the only opinions which he could find in those authorities if they were but fairly interpreted. The honesty and clarity with which his views were set out gave this book a large measure of its enormous influence: it would be hard to exaggerate its value or the strength of its impact on generations of readers eager to know what to believe and why to believe it.

*Knots Untied* in 1874 was followed by *Old Paths* in 1877; the two books were meant to complement each other. *Knots Untied* was designed to deal with the doctrinal issues which perplexed and troubled the Church; *Old Paths* was an exposition of "those leading doctrines of the Gospel which are generally necessary to salvation".[32]

Ryle was convinced that there are certain basic truths of which some knowledge is essential for salvation. Such truths are found in the Bible's teaching on sin, the cross, repentance. forgiveness, and on all the cognate issues which so greatly concern all who long to be right with God. "The longer I live the more I am convinced that the world needs no new Gospel," he wrote. " ... The same Gospel which was preached by Latimer and Hooper and Bradford, by Hall, Davenant, Usher, Reynolds and Hopkins, by Manton, Brooks, Watson, Charnock, Owen and Gurnall, by Romaine, Venn, Grimshaw, Harvey and Cecil: this is the Gospel which alone will do real good in the present day. The leading doctrines of that Gospel are the substance of the papers which compose this volume.... They are doctines which I find wear well, and in the faith of them I hope to live and die."[33]

But *Old Paths* was not his last book in that decade, for in November 1878 he published *Practical Religion* as a sequel to *Holiness* which had come out twelve months before. It dealt with "the daily duties, dangers, experience and privileges of all who profess and call themselves true Christians.... I think it will throw some light on what every believer ought to be, to do, and to expect."[34] There were chapters on such subjects as prayer, Bible reading, the Lord's Table, heirs to God, and eternity; written in plain, pithy language; and all designed to teach believers how to cultivate a walk with God.

Many authors of that generation were more brilliant than Ryle; there were few more deeply trusted as guides for those who were searchers for truth and pilgrims for God.

Ryle's words of good cheer at the end of a stormy decade were full of strong encouragement. "No doubt," he wrote in *The Churchman* whose first issue was published in January 1880, "the faults and infirmities of the Evangelical body are not few, and it does not need a Solomon to discern them.... But a calm review of our position affords strong reasons for thankfulness and encouragement. The Evangelical party with all its faults shows no symptoms of decay. We shall live and not die ... if we will only work and watch and pray and read and understand the times."[35]

Ryle was then sixty-three years old; he thought he would see out the rest of his days in Stradbroke. He was greatly taken aback when in March he was offered a fresh appointment as Dean of Salisbury. "I did not like it at all," he wrote. "I went to Salisbury, and the more I looked at it, the less I liked it. I wrote to my friends and asked them what I should do, and they all said I ought not to refuse it. They said it was my plain duty to go, and so, under pressure, I accepted."[36]

His appointment was immensely popular with fellow Evangelicals, but it never took effect. He had not left Stradbroke when he received an even more unexpected invitation to become the first Bishop of Liverpool, and this he immediately accepted.

As a result, on June 22nd, 1880, he preached for the last time as vicar of Stradbroke. So many people came for the evening service that extra seating had to be provided. As Ryle began to preach, he could not hide his feelings.

> The old street down which I walked so often, the school which I so often visited, the shops to which I have so often gone, the fields over which I have so often walked, the road with every yard of which I was so thoroughly acquainted, my own little garden in which I had meditation and prayer, my own little field shut out from the world where I have had quiet walks and communion with God, my own beautiful little church in which I have often seen so many faces – all these things I am about to leave and leave for ever. I go, called by God, to the noise, bustle, smoke and confusion of a great sea-port town . . . Pray for me, name me before the throne of grace and say, Lord God, bless Bishop Ryle.[37]

# BISHOP OF LIVERPOOL: 1880-1890

Liverpool on the north bank of the Mersey had been granted a charter by King John in 1205, but was little more than a small seaside village until the eighteenth century. It was transformed by the slave trade and then by the cotton imports, and its population had grown from seventy-seven thousand at the beginning of the nineteenth century to more than seven hundred thousand in the eighties. It had displaced Bristol as the second city in the kingdom and had become the first port in England. By 1850, its trade was double that of London; one out of ten ships in the world came from Liverpool; and the Mersey was soon to be dominated by six miles of docks.[1]

It was still part of the ancient see of Chester, but the movement for an independent jurisdiction in church affairs steadily gained in momentum during the seventies. The prime mover was John Torr, the member for Liverpool, and in December 1876, the Liverpool Bishopric Fund was started. Provision was made for the formation of a diocese by the Additional Bishoprics Act of 1878, and the Liverpool Bishopric Committee set out to raise one hundred thousand pounds as the minimum capital required for the endowment of the see.

John Torr was well aware of the very effective ministry which had been exercised by Frederic Barker at Edge Hill from 1827 to 1853 and had followed his career as Bishop of Sydney in New South Wales since 1854 with untiring interest. Sydney and her bishop were to have a small share in the formation of the see of Liverpool. "It was the work almost entirely of one man, her member, John Torr. And," wrote William Macquarie Cowper, "I have heard him say more than once that he was induced to undertake this work and to face the endless trouble which it involved, from seeing the great results which had been accomplished by Bishop Barker and other colonial prelates."[2]

Benjamin Disraeli, the Earl of Beaconsfield, had been Prime Minister since February 1874, but had suffered a crushing defeat at a general election in February 1880. He was nettled by the High Church vote for the Liberal Party and made up his mind to fill the several appointments to the house of Bishops before he laid down the seals of office.

The diocese of Liverpool was established by an Order in Council on March 24th to take effect as from April 19th. There is reason to think that he meant to recommend the appointment of James Fleming, the vicar of St. Michael's, Chester Square, as the bishop, but a strong deputation from Liverpool urged the need to appoint a man of strong Protestant convictions.

Algernon Turner, who was Beaconsfield's secretary, afterwards declared: "My recollection is that the choice lay between Ryle who had just been made a dean and Canon Fleming. Lord Beaconsfield inclined towards the latter, but my impression is that it was Lord Sandon who turned the scale."[3] The Prime Minister acquiesced and on April 10th wrote to the Queen: "The people of Liverpool are very anxious about their new bishop. The Tories subscribed the whole of the endowment and bought the palace. Lord Sandon says his seat for Liverpool depends upon the appointment being made by Your Majesty's present advisers. The whole city is most anxious that Your Majesty should appoint the present Dean of Salisbury, Canon Ryle."[4]

Strictly speaking, Ryle was still dean-elect and it was most unusual to bring his name forward for a different appointment at that juncture. Neither the Queen nor her

Prime Minister favoured Evangelicals as a rule, but they were not averse to making such an appointment for Liverpool where the Gladstones had strong family interests. Time was running out, but the Queen's reply gave her consent for an invitation to Ryle.

On Wednesday evening, April 16th, Ryle received a telegram from the Prime Minister's secretary, asking him to travel up to London the very next day for an interview on a very important matter. He did not know what it was all about, but went as a matter of plain duty.

At twelve o'clock on the Thursday, he saw Lord Sandon who told him that he had been sent for in order to ask him whether or not he would accept the Bishopric of Liverpool. Ryle was taken aback and said that he did not know what to say. Then Lord Sandon offered him an explanation. "We go out of office only next Monday, and when we go out of office, Mr. Gladstone may come in our place, and you must give us your answer as soon as you possibly can. You see if you don't make up your mind we will lose the Bishopric of Liverpool."

Ryle ventured to remind him that he was not so young as others. Lord Sandon brushed that aside. "We know all about that," he said, "we have made up our minds about that: the question is, will you take the Bishopric of Liverpool or not?" And Ryle gave his forthright reply: "My Lord, I will go." He asked a few questions and was then taken in to see Lord Beaconsfield. He told the Prime Minister that he was not so young as he once was. Lord Beaconsfield took a good look at him from head to foot and said: "I think, sir, you have a good constitution." And that was that. Ryle was later to say: "Salisbury took a week to think about, but to be Bishop of Liverpool did not take five minutes. I thought it was a clear, plain call of duty."

Ryle caught the train back to Stradbroke and told his wife: "I am Bishop of Liverpool." Word flashed through the village and the next day the bells were rung for joy.

On April 19th, letters patent were issued in connection with his appointment; three days later, Gladstone took office as Prime Minister.[5]

On April 26th, one week after his appointment was gazetted, Ryle went to Liverpool in order to meet the Bishopric Committee, and his intended attitude was made clear in the speech which he was called upon to make. "You know my opinions," he said. "I am a committed man. I come among you a Protestant and Evangelical: but I come with a desire to hold out the right hand to all loyal churchmen, holding at the same time my own opinions determinedly."[6]

Liverpool was jubilant: it had become a city; a new diocese had come into being; and Ryle had been chosen as its bishop. William Atkinson, a layman from Southport, was so delighted that he gave Ryle one thousand pounds for his removal expenses.[7] Richard Hobson, the vicar of St. Nathaniel's, declared that Ryle's appointment was "hailed with delight by every Evangelical Churchman throughout the world".[8]

The May meetings in London gave ample opportunity for the popular expression of this Evangelical enthusiasm. He was greeted at the annual meeting of the British and Foreign Bible Society "with loud and prolonged cheering",[9] and again at the annual meeting of the Church Missionary Society he was welcomed with a tumultuous ovation. "I thank you with all my heart," he said in response, "for the kind and flattering reception you have given me. I tried to hold the fort for Christ during the past thirty-five years in the comparative seclusion of Suffolk, and I hope by God's grace to hold the same fort in the giant city of Liverpool." Peter Toon says that the editorial writer for *The Record* was equally delighted and declared that Ryle's appointment was one of the best things Lord Beaconsfield had ever done for the Church of England.[10]

It was in this euphoric atmosphere that his consecration took place in York Minster on June 11th, 1880: the Archbishop of York was assisted by Lightfoot of Durham,

Jacobson of Chester, and Fraser of Manchester.

There were others in the Church of England who felt less than pleased at this turn of events. Lord Halifax, for example, the chairman of the Church Union, could let himself go with Henry Liddon and could indulge his pastime for overstating his views without fear of being misunderstood. He had caught wind of Ryle's appointment on April 17th and on that very day wrote to Liddon. "I must relieve my feelings," he said. "Canon Ryle Bishop of Liverpool! As I told Lord Devon last night, I rejoice beyond the expression of words that we have got rid of Lord Beaconsfield, Lord Cairns, and all their works, and only regret I did not stump the East Riding more than I did to turn out anyone who belongs to a party which in addition to its misdeeds is stupid enough to ignore what as Conservatives are their obvious relations to the Church. The Radicals may be bad, but at least they don't sin against the light. I declare I prefer Bradlaugh to Lord Beaconsfield, and I cannot say more... I am quite angry with Lord Devon... he is not angry about Canon Ryle!"[11]

*The Church Times* in a leader on July 2nd wrote in like vein:

We had hoped that by the time Bishop Ryle was consecrated he would at least have learned one episcopal virtue, that of holding his tongue; but in point of silly and indiscreet talk he has left even the most brilliant efforts of Bishop Ellicott far behind him. He has calmly informed the public that he was brought up as a man of fortune and was about to enter Parliament when his prospects were all changed by his father's bankruptcy; and the impression is suggested that like one of the descendants of Hophni and Phinehas, he must have said to some bishop, "Put me, I pray thee, into one of the priest's offices that I may eat a piece of bread."... He adds that he made up his mind about Liverpool in five minutes – that is to say, he was ready to thrust himself at a moment's notice into the most difficult of all the sees –

except perhaps London – simply because "that wonderful statesman" and that eminent Christian sage, the Earl of Beaconsfield, offered him the place.... We wish the Evangelical brethren joy of their champion.[12]

Ryle was enthroned in the provisional cathedral of St. Peter on July 1st and on the same day he sent out his first Pastoral Letter to the clergy. The last paragraph repeated what he had said to the Bishopric Committee on April 26th. "I ask you," he wrote, "to assist me by cultivating and encouraging a spirit of brotherly love, charity and forbearance among churchmen. In a fallen world like ours and in a free country like England, it is vain to expect all men to see things alike and to interpret the language of the formularies in the same way. Let us on no account be colourless churchmen destitute of any distinct opinions. But so long as any brother walks loyally within the limits of the Articles and her Prayer Book, let us respect him and treat him courteously even when we do not altogether agree with him."[13]

It was in this spirit that he took up his work in the newly created diocese; he was to strive through good report and ill report to be the just and patient friend of clergy and laymen alike. He chose as a motto for the new see the text: "Thy Word is truth" (John 17:17). Never before had he enjoyed so wide a scope for the proclamation of the Gospel, and his episcopal office did not for a moment spoil him as a preacher.

He had immense problems to face in a new see where there was no diocesan machinery at all; he had to lay essential foundations and build for the future from ground level. He determined to have an Archdeacon of Liverpool and an Archdeacon of Warrington and to ensure that the men who held each office were like-minded with him as conscientious Evangelicals. But he also had the right to appoint twenty-four honorary canons and he shared such appointments equally between Evangelicals and non-Evangelicals. Further, he set aside every Tuesday morning to meet and get to know some of his clergy, and so doing, he sought to place his finger on the pulse of the diocese.

The Diocese of Liverpool was the smallest in England except for London, but was packed with people who were largely uncared for by any adequate ministry. "If the Established Church of this country claims to be the Church of the people," Ryle said in his First Charge, "it is her bounden duty to see that no part of the people are left like sheep without a shepherd. If she claims to be a territorial and not a congregational Church, she should never rest till there is neither a street, nor a lane, nor a house, nor a garret, nor a cellar, nor a family, which is not regularly looked after and provided with the offer of the means of grace."[14]

Therefore his first concern was the need to provide for more living agents in the service of the Gospel. He had only one hundred and eighty-seven incumbents and one hundred and thirty-one curates to serve more than one million people: a striking contrast with the one thousand one hundred and sixty clergy for six hundred and sixty thousand people in the Diocese of Norwich.[15]

He toiled incessantly to build up the number of sound, well-trained clergy, and a steady increase took place from the outset of his episcopate. Within four years, the number of curates had increased from one hundred and thirty-one to one hundred and seventy.[16] But he set high standards for those who wished to be ordained and he would not license men from elsewhere who fell short in what he required. "I have not the least desire to lower the standard of requirements for the office of a deacon," he said, "and I cannot sympathise with those who press the bishops to bring into the ministry men who know little or nothing of Latin, Greek, Church History, the story of the English Reformation, the Prayer Book, the Church Catechism, or the Evidences of Christianity, and in short are only godly men who know the Bible and can talk about the Gospel."[17]

The need for more clergy never left him; its priority was never questioned. W.F. Machray could state that at the end of Ryle's episcopate, there were thirty-six more incumbents and one hundred and ten more curates than there had been in 1880: and that made up a total of four hundred and sixty-four licensed clergy in active work in the Diocese of Liverpool.[18]

But his efforts did not stop there. "The first thing needed," he said in 1881, "is not buildings, but living men – men ordained if you can get them, men not ordained if you can get no other agents; but in any case, men who have the grace of God and the love of souls in their hearts."[19] This led him well before many fellow bishops to use laymen as paid workers to complement the ministry of his clergy. He was able to build up the Scripture Readers' Society whose members were licensed to take services in Mission Rooms, to conduct Sunday Schools, and to visit the sick. He also established the Bible Women's Society whose members worked in the poorest districts and helped where the need was greatest. There were in all at the end of his episcopate forty-five Scripture Readers and thirty-one Bible women.[20] Further in 1882 he started the Voluntary Lay Helpers Association whose members grew in number to about five hundred and eighty and who worked in Sunday Schools and Bible Classes.

This steady growth in the number of clergy and lay workers made the need for more church buildings and mission halls imperative. "Out of the one hundred and eighty-seven consecrated churches in our new diocese," Ryle said in 1884, "no less than one hundred and thirty-seven have been built since the year 1880, and are churches practically without endowment, and dependent upon pew rents and voluntary offerings."[21] In his first five years as bishop, Ryle was able to consecrate no less than twenty-three entirely new churches; this number would increase to forty-two before the end of his episcopate.[22]

Ryle thought that not enough use was made of such church buildings. To erect a building at great cost and "then only use it four or five hours on Sunday, and perhaps four or five more during the week, does not appear to me

wise and sensible."[23] This led him to license mission halls
and school rooms for divine worship and to encourage their
erection "in order to attract and reach those who at present
go to no place of worship".[24] He thought they could be of
immense value for those who might shrink from a large
parish church but might be willing to attend a simple
elementary service in a room or a hall. Altogether forty-
eight mission halls were built and licensed before the year
1900.[25]

Clergy and lay workers were one great need; church
buildings and mission halls another: but what of a
cathedral? When Ryle was called upon to speak after his
consecration, he referred to the beauty of York Minster and
the need for a cathedral in the heart of Liverpool.[26] He was
far from indifferent to the various proposals under review,
but there were more urgent demands. "I only know," he
said in 1881, "that my first and foremost business ... is to
provide for preaching the Gospel to souls now entirely
neglected, whom no cathedral would touch."[27]

The Diocesan Conference in 1882 passed a resolution to
the effect that a cathedral must be built and a committee
was formed in 1883 to consider possible sites. "How many
times that committee has met," said Ryle in 1884, "and how
much anxious discussion has been devoted to the matter, I
will not attempt to say."[28] But a site was chosen and in 1885
the Liverpool Cathedral Act received royal assent. A
competition for the best design was won by William
Emerson and plans were drawn for a large Gothic building
which would have cost at least five hundred thousand
pounds.

But it was a time of financial recession; Ryle could not
see how to raise this sum of money; the three years allowed
by the Act expired; and that scheme died. "Our great
cathedral scheme makes no progress," Ryle said in 1889. "It
is on the shelf and sleeps for the present. I say 'sleeps'
advisedly: it is not dead, I hope, but sleeps."[29] It slept for a
long time and Ryle's patience wore thin. Thus in 1895, he
said: "It is rather trying... to be continually asked by

strangers, and even by men who are not strangers, When are you going to build a cathedral? No doubt a grand cathedral... would be an ornament to Liverpool and a beautiful luxury... In the meantime more clergy and more churches, within easy reach of every family, are a positive necessity in many of our overgrown parishes, and until they are provided, it is waste of time to talk of a cathedral."[30]

Ryle has been blamed for his failure to proceed with the construction of a cathedral, but he always felt that it was secondary in importance. He would have been glad to see it built if the large sum of money were there; failing that, he never ceased to feel that there were other priorities.

Ryle was anxious from the outset to maintain close contact with clergy and laymen, and to discuss diocesan needs and problems with them. For this purpose, he established a Diocesan Conference which met on a yearly basis from 1881 onwards.

Its normal meeting place was in St. George's Hall, a stately building in the centre of Liverpool. "It differs from all others, I believe, in one remarkable point," so Ryle said in 1887. "It is open to every licensed clergyman in the diocese, and is only elective for two lay representatives from each parish."[31] This was in line with the ideas which he had set out in 1871 before the first Diocesan Conference was held in Norwich.

Each conference began with an address by Ryle which took the form of a review of the current state of the Diocese; it then went on with Ryle's comments on the wider issues before the Church in matters both political and theological. This address was followed by a general discussion in which a frank exchange of views took place.

The conference had no legislative authority, but it was a step towards the kind of synodical government which had grown up in many colonial dioceses. It was supplemented by a triennial visitation when he addressed himself in a deliberate manner to his clergy.

The charge on such occasions stood by itself; there was no formal discussion. The first charge was divided into two sections and delivered at Liverpool and Wigan on October 19th and 20th, 1881. There were three more charges during his first ten years as a bishop: they were single utterances, all delivered in Liverpool as the see city, in 1884, 1887 and 1890. Ryle took great pains with each charge and strove to set out his views in a way that would both inform and educate the whole diocese so that no one could doubt where he stood or what he had in mind as he looked out on the Church of that day.

When Ryle was called upon to speak after his consecration in 1880, he had made the remark that "it is an easy matter to criticise the actions of bishops, but it is a far more difficult thing to be a bishop and to enter on the responsibilities of the appointment."[32] He was to meet criticism in plenty from papers like the *Mercury* and the *Courier*, the *Daily Post* and the *Echo*, and above all, the *Porcupine* and *Liberal Review*.

It had once been foretold that if he were ever made a bishop, there would be warm work in his diocese, and no quarter for his enemies.[33] He had returned the gift of a cope and mitre with thanks, saying that he would not make "a guy of himself".[34] When the choir in St. Paul's Cathedral turned to the east during the Creed in a service at which he was to preach, he bent forward so that all could see that he did not turn.[35]

Dean Church bluntly affirmed that Ryle's name was anathema to the Ritualist party. "The Bishop of Liverpool," so he wrote in February 1889, "is as obnoxious to all High Churchmen as the Bishop of Lincoln can be to any Low."[36] Ryle himself declared in his first triennial charge:

I venture to think that the present position of the Church of England is more critical and perilous than it has been at any period during the last two centuries. On every side the horizon is dark and lowring. There seem to be breakers ahead and breakers astern, dangers on the right hand and dangers on the left, dangers from without and dangers from within. Whether the good old ship will

weather the storm remains to be seen. But I am quite
certain that much depends, under God, on the conduct of
the crew. If reason and sanctified common sense prevail,
we shall live: if not, we shall die."[37]

How then would he handle clergy who were not of his
school in such matters as doctrine and worship? "I come to
the position I occupy as Bishop of Liverpool," he said,
"with a settled resolution to be just and fair and kind to
clergymen of every school of thought, whether High or
Low or Broad, or no party. To that resolution I mean to
adhere through evil report and good report."[38] But there
were some problems which he could not avoid.

His first visit to the Upper House of Convocation at
York was marked by a debate on the ornaments rubric in
the course of which Ryle observed that he had encountered
certain difficulties in his diocese. But he then went on to say
that he had refused requests for a prosecution because he
was convinced that a lawsuit would do more harm than
good.[39] This state of things prevailed until January 1885
when his hand was forced by certain events.

On January 21st, he consecrated the Church of St.
Agnes, built by Mr. Douglas Horsfall for the parish of
Toxteth, and known to be meant for High Church forms of
worship; he felt that he had no right to refuse on the basis
of what might take place but as yet had not occurred. The
more aggressive Protestant party in Liverpool was incensed
and on January 24th the *Protestant Standard* lamented
"the mournful death of Bishop Ryle's Evangelical and
Protestant principles".[40] They were hardly appeased when
Ryle refused to allow a Father Ignatius to hold a mission
on behalf of his monastery in any church in the diocese;
Father Ignatius simply took a hall in the city and carried on
for a fortnight.[41]

Therefore on January 29th, James Hakes, a leading
member of the Liverpool Church Association, resolved to
bring matters to a head by lodging a formal complaint
against the Rev. James Bell Cox who had become curate of

St. Margaret's Church in Princes Road, Liverpool, in 1869 and had been vicar since 1876. He was charged with violation of the law in respect of twelve distinct ceremonial matters in his conduct of the service of the Holy Communion. This left Ryle no alternative but to visit Bell Cox; the Archdeacon of Warrington and Ryle's legal secretary accompanied him in order to avoid all later misrepresentation. Ryle made a strong appeal to Bell Cox as his Father-in-God, but warned him as well that he did not feel free in conscience to veto all legal action. It was of no avail: Bell Cox would not accede in the slightest respect to his bishop's request.[42]

The Chancellor of Liverpool and the Archbishop of York both held that Ryle had no alternative but to allow the case to proceed unless Bell Cox would submit to the latest rulings of the Judicial Committee of the Privy Council. Bell Cox held that it would be an insult to his bishop to yield to a threat of prosecution when he had not yielded to the bishop's private appeal.

Ryle received two memorials, widely signed by clergy and laymen respectively, urging him to use the episcopal power of veto; but he addressed formal letters to Lord Penzance on March 6th, asking him to hear and resolve the case in the Chancery Court of York. His statement in reply to the Memorialists on March 7th explained his view of the matter. "Let me say," he wrote, "that I believe it has ever been a first principle of our country's constitution that every British subject who has a complaint to make against any person, whether clerical or lay, has a right to bring his complaint before those who administer the laws of the country. Believing this, I could not see, and cannot see, that it was my duty to debar the complainant against the Rev. J. Bell Cox from the exercise of this right. I do not enter into the merits of the case. I only say that to interfere between a person who charges another with breaking the law and a court of justice is to take up a position which I decline to adopt."[43] He went on to quote the words of the Lord Chief Justice as a member of the Royal Commission on

Ecclesiastical Courts. "I am very clearly of opinion," Lord Coleridge had said, "that the active interference of the bishops to prevent the law of the land being enforced against those who have broken it is as indefensible in theory as, I must confess, it seems to me to be fast becoming intolerable in practice."[44]

There is one brief sidelight on all this in Archbishop Benson's diary, and it has some value as an objective impression of Ryle: "Interview with Bishop of Liverpool as to his permitting the threatened ritual prosecution of Mr. B. He was very earnest and oppressed about it; seems to have tried honestly his best to avoid it. But these people like B. who are so excellent in theory of obedience, never obey a bishop even when he speaks of his own authority. The bishop had behaved magnanimously in consecrating a church for them. Without any sense of honour, the man immediately adopts all manner of illegal practice."[45]

Once it reached the law courts, the case passed out of Ryle's control. The court met in July and warned Bell Cox to cease from all illegal practices. Bell Cox would not acknowledge the court's jurisdiction and did not appear in person. He ignored its admonition with the result that in December he was suspended from office for six months for contempt of court and disobedience. Bell Cox took no notice of his suspension and in July 1886 Lord Penzance ordered his committal to prison. But this order was not acted upon at once as Bell Cox was able to deploy a series of technical, delaying tactics. At the Diocesan Conference that year, Ryle was to say: "The imprisonment of clergymen for contumacy is a relic of barbarism which ought to be swept away."[46] He did not name Bell Cox, but there could have been no doubt who was in his mind. He went on to refer to the violent criticism to which Bishop Fraser had been exposed because in similar circumstances he had acted on the great principle that justice must never be denied. Then Ryle added: "I am obliged to say that I have drunk a little of the same cup myself."[47]

At length on May 4th, 1887, Bell Cox was placed under

arrest and was put in Walton prison. He was released seventeen days later for technical reasons and that is where the matter ought to have been allowed to rest. But Hakes lodged an appeal and the court found in his favour; Bell Cox in turn appealed to the House of Lords and nine months later the House of Lords resolved that once any person had been released, even wrongfully, he could not be imprisoned again. The case thus came to an end in May 1888 and Bell Cox returned to St. Margaret's, Liverpool, to do just as he had done before.[48] But the complexities of the Bell Cox case left a scar on Ryle's heart that he would carry to the end of his life. He said little more in public, but there was a fleeting echo in his address to the Diocesan Conference in 1892: "The gravest defect," he said of the new Clergy Discipline Act, "is the retention of the episcopal veto, that most ingenious device for obliging a bishop to offend either one party or another in his diocese. However I know that in this matter I stand very much alone."[49]

Ryle's strong stand for the truth as he saw it was the stand of a man whose feet had been planted on that rock which no storm can shake. The new issues of *Knots Untied* which came out in 1885 and in 1896 contained a preface in which he declared: "The views which I held as a presbyter I still hold as a bishop."[50]

This was abundantly confirmed when he published as a sequel to *Knots Untied* his book entitled, *Principles For Churchmen: A Manual of Positive Statements on Doubtful or Disputed Points*. This book, which came out in 1884, was as significant as *Knots Untied* had been in its address to the mind and conscience of those whom he described as "true churchmen".[51] There were eighteen chapters in which he dealt with such subjects as the Church, the ministry, public worship, the Prayer Book, baptism and the Lord's Supper.

Ryle did not shirk controverted issues; he met them with bold and head-on debate. People might not agree with all his conclusions, but at least they were not left in doubt as to what he thought. This book was so frank and honest that it

soon came to share with *Knots Untied* a commanding
influence which continued unabated for years to come.

Then in 1887, he published *The Upper Room* in order to
bring together in one volume a number of sermons,
lectures, papers, pamphlets, which had appeared from time
to time over the years. "I have reached an age when I
cannot reasonably expect to write much more," he said in
the preface. "There are many thoughts in this volume which
I do not wish to leave behind me in the precarious form of
separate single sermons, addresses, lectures and tracts."[52]
So it did not contain freshly written material; it was indeed
neither more nor less than the truth when he confessed that
he was not likely to write much more. Here are sermons
preached before the Universities of Oxford and Cambridge
or in the Chapel Royal; here are chapters on regeneration
and the Lord's Supper; here, in particular, is Ryle's paper
on *Simplicity in Preaching*. It is like a vintage volume;
much of it is Ryle at his best; and it was a good note on
which to close.

# BISHOP OF LIVERPOOL: 1891-1900

The pace of life was to slow down as the nineties began to unfold. Mrs. Ryle had died in April 1889; this had left Ryle with a sense of loss and sorrow which time did little to abate. One brief sentence, written ten years later, within a year of his own death, draws the curtain aside for a fleeting moment: "Life has never been the same thing, or the world the same place, since my wife died."[1] She had brought a strength and comfort into his life which were sorely needed and had mothered her step-children with a warmth of love and understanding such as they could never adequately repay. She was buried at All Saints' Church, Childwall, and Ryle used to visit her grave each week whenever that was possible.

He had a large and loving heart, even though its beat was sometimes muffled under his cloak of high reserve. Nothing is known of his elder daughter, but Isabelle kept house for him after 1889 and served as his secretary as well. She of all the children had the closest affinity with her father in his spiritual outlook. On her death in 1921, Herbert wrote of her as "a very dear sister", one who was "a real good Christian girl and woman all her life,... a quite splendid secretary and factotum to my old father".[2]

Ryle's eldest son, Reginald, became a doctor, but seems to have had no Christian commitment at all. When he died in 1922, Herbert said that "he could not accept a faith, but his conduct was an example of fidelity, devotion and love".[3]

The youngest son was Arthur who became an artist: he

was "one of those happy, kindly souls who carry brightness with them wherever they go".[4] He died in March 1915 from cerebral meningitis contracted while he was engaged in war work at Felixstowe. Arthur did not share the same faith as his father, but Herbert described him as "the closest, most unselfish and loving of brothers".[5] Herbert was to write in 1922 after Reginald's death: "The last of us five, I remain, having had two such loving brothers as few men ever had – never a quarrel, always affection and confidence."[6]

Ryle's middle son, Herbert, had become a fellow of King's College, Cambridge, and was ordained in 1882. Ryle followed his activities with an interest and an affection which nothing could impair. "If anything like coolness or want of confidence ever arose between us," he had once written, "it would break my heart."[7] It gave him great joy when Herbert became Hulsean Professor of Divinity in 1888 and President of Queens' College in 1896, and the only shadow between father and son was the fact that Herbert had now become one of the most influential scholars in the field of Old Testament Higher Criticism. This gulf in their outlook was marked in the first line of a letter which the younger Ryle wrote from the Bishop's Palace in Abercromby Square: "I write in a land where antagonistic German criticism has not obtained much foothold, even in the bookshelves."[8]

When *Lux Mundi* was published in 1889, Dean Church made a significant remark: "Things are no doubt changed, and the bishops are changed, and most of them, except perhaps Liverpool, accept as truisms what their ignorant predecessors held up to execration."[9] Ryle held his old views with unshakable tenacity, but not for one moment were they allowed to cloud the trust and love between father and son. "Much as he differed from me in many points," Herbert wrote after his death, "he never suffered the shadow of a difference to come between us";[10] and the treasured intimacy of confidence and affection was to grow to the end. Letters from Ryle were crammed with the details of his life and activity, while visits from Herbert always brought him supreme content.

Ryle did not live to share in the joy of Herbert's later career: he was consecrated as Bishop of Exeter in January 1901 and was translated to the Diocese of Winchester in April 1903. He was installed as Dean of Westminster Abbey in April 1911 and held that office until his death in August 1925. There is one revealing entry in the diary which he kept from time to time: "May 10, 1916: Centenary of my dear old Father's birthday! how continually one's thoughts go back to him!"[11]

Ryle was seriously ill in 1891; he made a good recovery, but his physical stamina had been reduced. This led him to appoint the Right Rev. Peter Sorenson Royston, formerly a missionary, then Bishop of Mauritius, as an assistant bishop in the Diocese of Liverpool.

He delivered his fifth triennial charge in November 1893: it proved to be the last. He had come to attach a much greater significance to the Diocesan Conference; this was maintained each year until 1898.

The cathedral project had reached a stalemate as he told the Diocesan Conference in 1897: "The unsuccessful attempt to provide a cathedral worthy of our new diocese at the beginning of my episcopate, and the many weary committee meetings at the Town Hall about the subject, are now matters of ancient history, and many people seem totally ignorant of them. I take occasion to remark that I was present at all those meetings, and the common slanderous report that the bishop took no interest in the subject and did not wish a cathedral to be built, is destitute of a grain of truth."[12] Continuing disagreement as to a site and the formidable sum of money required had convinced him that it would proceed no further in that generation.

This had led him as far back as 1889 to say that what was most needed was a diocesan Church House which would provide necessary accommodation for all administrative purposes and would make Liverpool independent of Chester.[13] Once the cathedral scheme was abandoned, his mind was made up. "From then on," he said, "I resolved to promote the erection of a Church House, and after long delay caused by bad times, I have lived to see the keel laid."[14] That was in 1897 when a site became available. Ryle lived to see the foundation stone laid in 1899, but the building was not opened until 1901.

Ryle's will was to convey his huge library to the diocese: this was his most treasured earthly possession. Church House with all Ryle's books and the diocesan records was destroyed in 1941 as the result of an air raid. But a catalogue of all his books had been printed and copies still exist in the Liverpool University Library and the City Central Library.[15]

Ryle looked back in November 1897 with great thankfulness for all that God had brought to pass. "I began my episcopate with one hundred and seventy incumbents," he said; "there are now two hundred and five. I began with one hundred and twenty curates; there are now two hundred and twenty. In my first year I had four thousand five hundred young persons presented to me for confirmation; in 1896 I had eight thousand three hundred. I should be very ungrateful if I did not thank God every day for these undeserved mercies."[16]

He had felt a special concern for the inadequate stipends of his clergy in the eighties: this led him in 1891 to launch a Diocesan Sustentation Fund which raised the value of the poorest living to a minimum salary of two hundred and fifty pounds per annum. His next step was to set up a Diocesan Clergy Pension Fund which made retirement possible for all clergy when their working days were over. Both funds were based on the pattern evolved by Thomas Chalmers in Scotland, and both were new ventures in the Church of England.

Ryle held an annual reunion for all whom he had ordained to the priesthood: there were about one hundred and sixty clergy at the last reunion in January 1899. "Nothing could be more delightful than the genial loving manner of the bishop," so Richard Hobson wrote of these occasions, "or more helpful than his wise fatherly counsel."[17]

Richard Hobson was perhaps Ryle's closest friend among the clergy and St. Nathaniel's Church, where Hobson served from 1864 to 1901, was the church in which Ryle and his family used to worship. Hobson had begun with a cellar meeting of five people; when he retired, there was an average attendance on Sundays of two thousand.[18] This was parish work that Ryle knew how to value. He told the Church Congress at Derby in 1882 how he had helped to distribute the bread and wine to three hundred and ninety-five communicants in St. Nathaniel's: "I saw the hands which received them, and I know by those hands that many of them were dock-labourers and foundry men."[19]

In the spring of 1884, Ryle had spoken to men from the coal-yards in the parish hall. They cheered him when he came and when he went, "for he had already made his mark amongst the working people of the city by his terse homely style of speaking and the practical nature of his strong, sound common-sense utterances." "Indeed," said Hobson, "he might well have been styled the working man's bishop."[20]

Ryle would not act as a party bishop in the conduct of his diocesan duties, but he never ceased to be a party leader in the Church as a whole. The fact that he was on the bench gave new heart to Evangelicals at a time when they were reeling before the twin assaults of Ritualism and Liberalism. Between 1889 and 1891, *The Record* published a number of letters which had been signed as from "An Old Soldier" or "A Northern Churchman": two *noms de plume* which masked the same author, and that author, as all men knew from the terse and trenchant English, was none other than Ryle.[21]

He was deeply perturbed when the Judicial Committee of the Privy Council upheld Benson's judgement on the Lincoln case in 1892: a far-reaching verdict which gave legal sanction for the very things which all Evangelicals had hoped it would condemn. What the Gorham judgment of 1850 had done for Evangelicals or the Essays and Reviews judgment of 1864 for Liberals, the Lincoln judgment had now done for Ritualists. It marked the end of the road for the Church Association in its long fight through the courts to outlaw, or at least to restrain, the progress of Ritualism in a Rome-ward direction.

Ryle took as grave a view of the case as the most anxious of his brethren, but he would not allow anyone to panic while the fundamentals remained secure. He had raised his voice times without number to urge fellow churchmen not to despair when they saw with growing dismay how the Church was changing before their eyes. This new crisis called forth a new exhortation from "that man of wise and single heart", as H.C.G. Moule so fitly called him.[22] "I charge my brethren," so Ryle wrote to *The Record* in August 1892, "not to listen for a moment to those who counsel secession from the Church of England; I have no sympathy with the rash and impatient men who recommend such a step. So long as the Articles and Prayer Book are not altered, we are in an impregnable position; we have an open Bible, and our pulpits are free."[23]

Ryle had always taken the view that church reform should accompany church defence. He had declared his mind on this matter very clearly at the Diocesan Conference in 1885. "We must try to rectify known abuses, to stop the sale of livings, to revive ecclesiastical discipline, to simplify our Prayer-book services, to proportion revenues to duties, to provide pensions for aged or infirm clergymen, to organise a system of aggressive evangelisation for overgrown or neglected parishes, and to give the laity their rightful place in all the Councils of the Church."[24]

He sought to walk in the old paths with an unshaken confidence throughout his last decade. "Our honoured fathers in the last century, Romaine and Berridge and Grimshaw and the elder Venn, had far greater difficulties around them than we have," he wrote in 1892; "but they stood firm and held their ground. Let us do likewise."[25] Nevertheless he was gravely disturbed by clergy who wanted a mass and an altar and a confessional in their churches, and such developments in the Church of England troubled him more deeply than the strongest attacks launched from outside.

In 1897, he refused to license a curate for the parish of St. Thomas, Toxteth, because the would-be curate taught auricular confession.[26] In August 1898, he issued a letter to his clergy on "lawlessness" in the conduct of church worship, charging them to abstain from such things as incense, lighted candles, sacrificial vestments, the use of the word "mass", regular confession and the reserved sacrament.[27] One more important article on this subject appeared in a number of daily papers some time after Benson's death in 1896, and the tone of his voice had lost none of its ring in his last words: "Some people, I know, regard these things as trifles. I can not see with their eyes. They are very mischievous trifles. They are just the kind of things which in the present day are gradually sapping the foundations of the Church of England. They irritate and annoy the lower middle classes who can not find them in the very Prayer Book which from childhood they have been urged to value and treat with veneration... If they continue to increase and are not checked, the end will be disestablishment, disendowment, and disruption. This at any rate is my deliberate opinion."[28]

Herbert Ryle at the close of his life told his son: "You know we Ryles are very reserved in some ways."[29] It was a simple but revealing utterance, and it applied to John Charles Ryle as much as to his son. Ryle was always forthright, authoritative, enthusiastic, a man who made a strong impact on his congregation. People saw him as a man of commanding appearance, and that air of patrician dignity helped to cast its own kind of spell. But his very height gave him a touch of hauteur which made him seem somewhat aloof in his personal relations. This hid his real warmth of heart from many who were outside his own intimate family circle.

Perhaps to some extent he was conscious of this, for he tried hard to reach out with goodwill to men on all levels of life. He knew that no Church on earth is perfect, and no churchman in this world is free from sin and error. Therefore he held out the hand of friendship to clergy and laymen alike, even though they were men from whom in some matters he might widely differ, and his personal relations with some who held "advanced" ideas had all the marks of "warm humanity".[30] He went out of his way to show kindness to some who could see little to like either in the man or in his episcopate. He tried to treat all his clergy with an unaffected belief in their sincerity and to value their work for its own sake without regard to mere party motive. "He was tolerant to a degree little known or recognised," so his son wrote after his death; "the High Church writers deliberately sought to destroy his position by detraction."[31]

It was clear that towards the end of his episcopate, he had won the goodwill of some who at first had shown scant respect.[32] "Bold as a lion for the truth," said Richard Hobson after his death, "he was yet tender even to those who could not see anything good in him or in his work as a bishop."[33] It is doubtful whether any Victorian bishop gave his people such clear spiritual leadership as did Ryle, and on balance it may safely be said that when he laid down his office, the Diocese of Liverpool was one of the best organised sees in England.

Ryle's health in the nineties was such that he could no longer travel as widely or often as he had done in the eighties. He went to a Church Congress for the last time in 1890, and he had to decline journeys to London unless for a special purpose. But he retained all his concern for the great church bodies with which he had for so long been identified and his pen was always ready to state his views with the trenchant vigour which all men knew. He was under special obligation as a bishop in the Northern Province to attend the Convocation of York, and the records reveal the fact that he took his full share in the debates.[34]

He had become a member of the House of Lords in 1884, but his attendance was minimal: he did not take part in political debate, and he only went when it was his turn to read the prayers. He spoke of a meeting of the bishops which was held in London as weak, evasive, impotent. "I came away vexed and annoyed," he told Herbert, "and am not at all disposed to go up again to London for one night for such a waste of time."[35]

He had not gone to the Lambeth Conference in 1888, but became involved in controversy when its Encyclical Letter was published. This letter contained the famous Lambeth Quadrilateral as a basis for union with other Churches; Ryle felt that it papered over differences about Scriptures and doctrine within the Church of England.

Nor was he able to attend the Conference in 1897 because of illness, but he returned to his former criticism.

I cannot refrain from expressing one general opinion. I must deeply regret that the Lambeth Conference completely ignored and passed over the "unhappy divisions", both about doctrine and ritual, of the Church of England in the present day. They are divisions which threaten to undo the work of the Reformation and are gradually rending the Established Church into two distinct parties, and destroying the peace of families, parishes and congregations. No doubt a cautious policy of silence in the Conference about these divisions saved much trouble, prevented awkward collisions and made things work smoothly. But... I can not refrain from saying... that in my opinion this policy of silence was not really wise.[36]

Ryle was at heart an evangelist whose sermons always sounded the note of a singularly clear call to forgiveness of sin and acceptance with God. Richard Hobson's comment after Ryle had preached in St. Nathaniel's on the first Sunday in 1885 is an illustration: the Gospel was proclaimed, he said, "with a freshness and a power that sent us on our way rejoicing".[37]

Ryle had always had a warm heart for the American Evangelist, D.L. Moody, and had written of him in May 1875: "I can thoroughly understand the theology of Moody and Sankey, and go along with it entirely."[38] In 1883, he welcomed Moody and Sankey to Liverpool and declared that he was "one of those who thank God extremely for Mr. Moody".[39] And in July 1892, Moody agreed to speak on the Sunday evening at Keswick after the Convention had come to an end. Ryle went with him and they stood on the platform side by side: Ryle led the meeting in prayer and Moody gave the address.[40]

Then in 1895, Ryle sponsored the Liverpool General Christian Mission when the Rev. W. Hay Aitken and Prebendary W.E. Askwith were the evangelists. At the Diocesan Conference in November that year, he publicly expressed his thankfulness for all that God had done for the city in that mission.[41] And in 1896, the Student Volunteer Missionary Society held a conference in Liverpool. Douglas Thornton was one of the leaders; there were about one thousand students present; C.T. Studd and George Pilkington brought field reports; and Ryle gave the inaugural address. "If you go forth in the name of the Lord Jesus," he said, "armed with the Word of God and holding the truth of the everlasting Gospel, . . . I can not doubt that the good seed will bear abundant fruit, although you may not live to see it."[42]

Ryle always had pleasant relationships with the Non-Conformist Churches and in 1898 he entertained the President of the Methodist Conference at the palace. "If we cannot remove the hedges that separate us," he said, "let us keep them as low as we can and shake hands over them."[43] Moody died at Northfield on December 22nd, 1899. He had said as the day began: "Earth recedes; heaven opens before me."[44] Ryle would understand; six months later, heaven would open for him also.

Ryle did not sit alone on the episcopal bench as an Evangelical, and he took a natural interest in the various appointments to vacant sees. This led to a curious connection with the appointment of a successor to Frederic Barker for the Diocese of Sydney.

Barker died in April 1882, and the Diocesan Synod, in

consultation with committees of the provincial bishops and the bishops of Australia and Tasmania, asked five English bishops to put forward the name of one person whom the committee would accept or reject. The five English bishops were Edward White Benson of Canterbury, William Thomson of York, Joseph Barber Lightfoot of Durham, Anthony Thorold of Rochester and John Charles Ryle of Liverpool. Ryle and Thorold were decidedly Evangelical; Thomson and Lightfoot were sympathetic.

It is impossible to know what consultation took place in England, but the outcome was that the five English bishops sent the name of the Rev. Canon Alfred Barry, Principal of King's College, London. The joint committees then met in Sydney and confirmed Barry's appointment. He was consecrated in Westminster Abbey on January 1st, 1884 and arrived in Sydney to be enthroned on April 24th. But it was a strange choice for a diocese which had become so resolutely Evangelical in character under Bishop Barker. He was a Broad Churchman who cared little for church parties and who advocated what he conceived of as the wise comprehension of all schools of thought and all forms of worship in the Church of England. His name had been rejected at an earlier stage in the Diocesan Synod, and one cannot see how Ryle in particular came to give his consent to the nomination.[45] It was an experience which made him ultra cautious and may partly explain his strong opposition in 1896 to the appointment of a non-Evangelical to the Diocese of Osaka which was staffed by the Church Missionary Society.[46]

He wrote to Lord Salisbury from time to time on the ground that the Diocese of Liverpool had returned no less than seventeen Conservatives at one election, and he urged the claims of certain men, not without success, for some senior appointment. Among them were William Lefroy who became Dean of Norwich and Henry Wace who became Dean of Canterbury, J.W. Diggle who became Bishop of Carlisle and H.C.G. Moule who became Bishop of Durham.[47]

In 1889, Ryle was asked to address the Islington Clerical Conference on the subject of the Lord's Supper. He had already included chapters on this subject in *Knots Untied*, *Principles for Churchmen*, and *The Upper Room*; the angles of approach and the content of each chapter had varied, but the basic treatment in each case was the same. Now once more he was called upon to handle this subject and he did so as a solemn duty.

He began by saying: "I can only present old things in a new light."[48] His address was subsequently printed with the title, *What Is Written About The Lord's Supper?* It is a fifty-page pamphlet in which he set out to answer two main questions: What does the New Testament teach about the Lord's Supper, and what does the New Testament not teach about the Lord's Supper? It was as fearless and forthright in its declaration of truth as he was ever wont to be; and it was the last time that he drew up such a paper with a view to publication.

There was nothing further bearing his name until 1900 when *The Christian Race and Other Sermons* appeared. This was like a book born out of due time, but it gave the Church an example of the kind of sermon Ryle loved to preach. Then in 1903 one more book came out in the form of a posthumous collection of his major diocesan utterances. It was entitled *Charges and Addresses* and it bound up in one volume his five triennial visitation charges from 1881 to 1893 and eight Diocesan Conference addresses from 1885 to 1898.

There were also a sermon preached in Liverpool in 1889, and an address at the Hull Church Congress in 1890. Copies of this volume were hard to find, but in 1978 the Banner of Truth Trust brought out a new edition. This left out a sermon on the Royal Jubilee in 1887, but included Ryle's "Farewell to the Diocese" written on February 1st, 1900.[49] This volume is as invaluable for a knowledge of Ryle's episcopate as the autobiography is for details of his life up to the year 1860. So ended Ryle's contribution as an author: what he wrote stands written for all who will read today.

The historian, E.L. Woodward, has observed that Simeon and Wilberforce had no successors of like calibre in the generation after their death.[50] But this verdict overlooks the role of Lord Shaftesbury of whom it could be said that "by 1840 he had emerged as not merely the leading Evangelical layman, but as the only real leader of a party which was at this period lacking in outstanding or distinguished clergy".[51] It was only in the sixties that Ryle began to come to the fore, but by the time of Shaftesbury's death in 1885, his leadership was acknowledged by all Evangelical churchmen.

Ryle was, in fact, a born leader of men and a humble servant of God whose courage was equal to the day of trouble and whose calm faith brought new hope to those who watched with anxious eyes as the sky seemed to darken over the Church. He was singularly immune from the narrow outlook and the bitter feeling which so often have their roots in controversy, and "the stark black and white of his bluntly expressed writings" may do less than justice to the genuine courtesy which was one of his great virtues.[52]

Earlier misfortune might have soured his spirit and left the scar of a lasting grievance; it did, in fact, result in a feeling of injury and resentment which was not healed until after he had moved to Stradbroke. It made him brusque and proud and aloof for years, reserved in society because haunted by adversity. But the grace of God had broken through that mask of iron restraint and had brought out a more gentle spirit to match his strength. His work was not without its errors and mistakes, but they were not allowed to cloud his mind. "I have had too many failures in my own life," he told Herbert, "and seen too many, to dwell on failures long."[53]

During the last twenty years of the long Victorian era, Ryle stood head and shoulders above men of his day as a leader *par excellence* in times of great uncertainty. "It is no exaggeration to say," Mr. Albert Mitchell wrote in 1941, "that his virile personality dominated two generations of Evangelicals and set its ineradicable mark upon a third."[54]

The Ryles had grown to love the Lake District in the north of England and the mists and moors of the Scottish Highlands. Their holidays for many years were divided between Keswick and Pitlochry.

Catherine Marsh went to the Keswick Convention for the first time in 1890 and kept up her visits each year until 1910. Her old friendship with Ryle was renewed fifty years after his ordination and she described an afternoon which she had spent with Ryle and his daughter in their lovely home at Skiddaw. "Before we left," she told a friend, "he prayed with us, such a patriarchal, patriotic and personal prayer."[55]

Ryle had been ill both in 1872 and in 1891, but his splendid physique showed few real signs of wear until the last phase of his life. Thus in 1895, he told Herbert: "I am a wonder to myself in my ability to do so much without fatigue."[56] Richard Hobson was to record that in 1898 Ryle took his last confirmation in St. Nathaniel's with his usual energy: "He was just his own self in his address, and in his usual tone. The church was not able to hold all who came to it."[57]

But the wheels of life were slowing down as the year 1899 began. On January 8th he preached at St. Nathaniel's for the last time, choosing as his text the words of the Lord Jesus: "I pray not that Thou shouldest take them out of the world, but that Thou shouldest keep them from the evil" (John 17:15). "The discourse," wrote Richard Hobson, "was marked by well-nigh his usual strength and vigour. Truly, whenever he came to us, he brought a blessing with him."[58] Then in April, he was in the chair at Queen's Hall for one of the centenary meetings of the Church Missionary Society. It was virtually his last public meeting, and he received a great personal ovation.[59]

He was very low that summer but went with his daughter to his favourite resort at Lowestoft in July. Herbert came to visit him there and found him "so evidently enfeebled in step, hearing, and memory" that he took upon himself the delicate task of advising his father to resign from the see.[60]

Ryle was relieved to receive this advice and made up his mind to resign in the new year. Meanwhile he returned to Liverpool, but was able to do very little in the latter part of 1899. Bishop Royston carried out most of his duties and he seldom left the palace.

But on Christmas Day he came once more to St. Nathaniel's; Richard Hobson described it all.

As we were about to commence the 11 o'clock service on Christmas Day, a tap was heard at the vestry entrance to the church, and on the door being opened, to our utter amazement there was the bishop, quite bent, with his family, including the present Bishop of Winchester. They all sat in the vicar's pew. The bishop as was his custom sat in the corner where good Mrs. Ryle used to sit. The congregation was visibly affected at seeing their dear bishop, always so straight and commanding, now bowed down . . . At the Sacrament, the bishop came to the rail, followed by his children who knelt on either side of him. For a moment I felt almost overcome; which he must have perceived, for looking up at me, he said softly, "Go on". They remained till the congregation had gone, when I went to him. He reached out his poor hand and drew me to him, saying, "This is the last time; God bless you; we shall meet in heaven". The big tears trickled down his furrowed cheeks.[61]

Hobson went to bid him goodbye in January 1900. Ryle gave him the Bible which he had used for more than fifty years and then offered what he called a parting prayer. "I knelt by his chair," wrote Hobson, "and oh, what a prayer he offered for me! I shall never forget it."[62] He had used up all his reserves of strength and on February 1st he addressed a farewell letter to the diocese. "I can truly say that my approaching separation from Liverpool will be a heavy wrench to me," he wrote. "I shall never forget you. I had ventured to hope that I might be allowed to end my days near the Mersey and to die in harness. But God's thoughts are not as our thoughts, and He has gradually taught me by failing health that the huge population of this diocese requires a younger and stronger bishop."[63] And he ended by saying: "In a little time we shall all meet again; many I hope on the King's right hand and few on the left. Till that time comes ... I remain your affectionate bishop and lasting friend, J.C. Liverpool."[64]

His resignation took effect on March 1st and he and his daughter moved from Liverpool to Lowestoft a week or two later. He had bought a pleasant house overlooking the North Sea. Only a few weeks of life still remained; his strength was spent. On June 9th, he was only partly conscious and his daughter called the doctor and sent for her brothers. Only Herbert was able to arrive in time, for on Sunday, June 10th, in the eighty-fifth year of his age, Ryle was summoned to his reward. There was no pain; the end was calm: but for Herbert, it was "a blow to which nothing can be compared".[65] Eighteen months later, he wrote to a friend: "The father is the background of life: and when he is taken, the world looks a different place ... It never can be the same. This is ... only the very fresh recollection of my own experience last year when my father died."[66]

Ryle was buried beside his wife at All Saints' Church, Childwall, on the slope of a hill looking south across the Mersey into Cheshire. "The church," so Herbert wrote, "was filled with clergy and gentry. The graveyard was crowded with poor people who had come in carts and vans and buses to pay the last honours to the old man who certainly had won their love."[67] The gravestone was engraved with two texts of which the second was a deliberate reminder of his conversion: "By grace are ye saved through faith" (Eph. 2:8).

Hobson was the ordinary preacher at the provisional cathedral for the afternoon service on Sunday, June 17th.

Ryle, he said, "was great through the abounding grace of God. He was great in stature; great in mental power; great in spirituality; great as a preacher and expositor of God's most holy Word; great in hospitality; great in winning souls to God; great as a writer of Gospel tracts; great as an author of works which will long live... great as first Bishop of Liverpool. I am bold to say that perhaps few men in the nineteenth century did so much for God, for truth, for righteousness, among the English speaking race and in the world as our late bishop."[68] And no finer tribute could have been paid than in one brief phrase of Bishop Chavasse who spoke of him as "that man of granite with the heart of a child".[69]

# WORKS BY J.C. RYLE

1. 1849 *Spiritual Songs.*
2. 1850 *Hymns for the Church on Earth.*
3. 1854 *The Bishop, The Pastor,* and *The Preacher.*
4. 1856 *Expository Thoughts on The Gospel of St. Matthew* (my copy 1896).
5. 1857 *Expository Thoughts on The Gospel of St. Mark* (my copy 1896).
6. 1858 *Expository Thoughts on The Gospel of St. Luke* (Vol.1) (my copy 1896).
7. 1859 *Expository Thoughts on The Gospel of St. Luke* (Vol.2) (my copy 1896).
8. 1859 *Home Truths* (seven volumes).
9. 1868 *Bishops and Clergy of Other Days.*
10. 1868 *Christian Leaders of England in the Last Century* (my copy 1868).
11. 1868 *We Must Unite.*
12. 1871 *A Churchman's Duty about Diocesan Conferences.*
13. 1873 *Expository Thoughts on The Gospel of St. John* (three volumes) (my copy 1896).
14. 1873 A fragment of autobiography (1816-1860) (Edited by Peter Toon with the title, *J.C. Ryle: A Self-Portrait,* Reiner Publications, 1975).
15. 1874 *Knots Untied* (my copy 1898).
16. 1877 *Old Paths* (my copy 1884).
17. 1877 *Holiness* (my copy 1879).
18. 1877 *What Do We Owe to the Reformation?* (my copy 1877).

19.  1878  *Practical Religion* (my copy 1883).
20.  1882  *Simplicity in Preaching* (my copy 1882).
21.  1884  *Principles For Churchmen* (my copy 1884).
22.  1887  *The Upper Room* (my copy 1888).
23.  1889  *What Is Written About The Lord's Supper?* (my copy 1889).
24.  1890  *Light From Old Times* (my copy 1890).
25.  1900  *The Christian Race and Other Sermons* (my copy 1900).
26.  1903  *Charges and Addresses* (my copy, The Banner of Truth Trust edition, 1978).


# BOOKS OF REFERENCE

1.  1900  W.F. Machray, *The Right Reverend John Charles Ryle*.
2.  1903  Richard Hobson, *What Hath God Wrought?*
3.  1909  Arthur R.M. Finlayson, *The Life of Canon Fleming*.
4.  1917  J.M. Rigg, "John Charles Ryle" *(Dictionary of National Biography*, Vol. XXII, Supplement 1917).
5.  1928  Maurice H. Fitzgerald, *A Memoir of Herbert Edward Ryle*.
6.  1941  Albert Mitchell, "John Charles Ryle" *(The Record*, July 11th, 1941).
7.  1947  M. Guthrie Clark, *John Charles Ryle*.
8.  1949  E.D.H. Tollemache, *The Tollemaches of Helmingham and Ham*.
9.  1963  G.W. Hart, *Bishop J.C. Ryle, Man of Granite*.
10.  1967  M.L. Loane, *Makers of Our Heritage* (chapter one).
11.  1976  Peter Toon and Michael Smout; *John Charles Ryle, Evangelical Bishop*.

12. 1977 J.S. Reynolds, "Towards A Full Treatment" *(English Churchman,* June 3rd, 1977).
13. 1978 John Kent, *Holding The Fort, Studies in Victorian Revivalism.*

## OTHER SOURCES

1. 1855 Frederic Barker, Bishop of Sydney, Manuscript diaries.
2. 1855 Mrs. Barker, Manuscript diaries and letters.
3. 1882 W. Knight, *Memoir of Henry Venn.*
4. 1888 W.M. Cowper, *Episcopate of the Right Rev. Frederic Barker ... A Memoir.*
5. 1894 Mary A. Church, *The Life and Letters of Dean Church.*
6. 1896 J.C. MacDonnell, *The Life and Correspondence of William Connor Magee, Archbishop of York.*
7. 1899 A.C. Benson, *Edward White Benson.*
8. 1899 Eugene Stock, *The History of the Church Missionary Society.*
9. 1901 H.C.G. Moule, *The Evangelical School in The Church of England.*
10. 1906 J.W. Diggle, *Quiet Hours With The Ordinal.*
11. 1908 G.R. Balleine, *A History of The Evangelical Party in the Church of England* (my copy, 1951 new edition).
12. 1909 Eugene Stock, *My Recollections.*
13. 1910 F. Warre Cornish, *The English Church in the Nineteenth Century.*
14. 1913 W.H. Griffith Thomas, *The Work of the Ministry.*
15. 1917 L.E. O'Rorke, *The Life and Friendships of Catherine Marsh.*

16. 1929   J.B. Lancelot, *Francis James Chavasse, Bishop of Liverpool.*
17. 1935   G.L. Prestige, *The Life of Charles Gore.*
18. 1935   J.G. Lockhart, *Charles Lindley, Viscount Halifax.*
19. 1938   E.L. Woodward, *The Age of Reform, 1815-1870.*
20. 1947   H. Gresford Jones, *F.J. Chavasse.*
21. 1953   J.C. Pollock, *A Cambridge Movement.*
22. 1963   J.C. Pollock, *Moody Without Sankey.*
23. 1964   J.C. Pollock, *The Keswick Story.*
24. 1966   David Newsome, *The Parting of Friends.*
25. 1974   Georgina Battiscombe, *Shaftesbury, 1801-1885.*
26. 1976   M.L. Loane, *Hewn from the Rock* (Moorhouse lectures).

# VALE

I bless Thee for the quiet rest Thy servant taketh now;
  I bless Thee for his blessedness, and for his crownèd
    brow;
For every weary step he trod in faithful following Thee,
  And for the good fight foughten well, and closed right
    valiantly.

*Mrs. A. Stuart-Menteith*

# APPENDIX

# THE DISTINCTIVE CHARACTER OF EVANGELICAL TESTIMONY

Those who rejoice to call themselves Evangelicals, as did John Charles Ryle, will do well to look to the rock from which they were hewn and to come to terms with what is meant by that name. It is used so widely, so freely, so glibly, that one sometimes wonders what its significance is for those who use it. It should never be a mere party label, used in partisan hostility to those who are non-Evangelical. That might suit old-fashioned Low Churchmen, but it is a parody of what that designation ought to mean.

The word "Evangelical" has a long and honourable history. Its theology is rooted in the New Testament and places its emphasis on its most salient doctrines. Its tradition moulded the Reformation theology of the sixteenth century and the Puritan leadership of the seventeenth century; the spiritual awakening of the eighteenth century and the Victorian seriousness of the nineteenth century. Its strength has always been in the middle classes: it has never had so firm a hold on the upper social echelon or in the poorer wage-earning community. It was Evangelical faith and vision which led to the wonderful revival of missionary enterprise and sent men and women in their hundreds to the ends of the earth in the Name of Christ. It was Evangelical love and concern which awoke the conscience of England to human sorrow and tragedy at home and overseas. And the underlying strength and motive for all Evangelical initiative are the four great basic doctrines which command a distinctive emphasis in Evangelical faith and testimony.

What are these primary doctrines? They are, first, the integrity and authority of Holy Scripture as the Word of God; secondly, the fact of justification as an act of grace by faith alone; thirdly, the forgiveness of sins on the sole ground of Christ's death on the cross; fourthly, the absolute necessity of the new birth by the Holy Spirit. Others may hold the same doctrines in more or less degree; but for the Evangelical, they have particular significance and are crucial for his understanding of the Gospel.

## 1. *The integrity and authority of Holy Scripture as the Word of God.*

The Old Testament is the foundation of the Bible as a revelation of the character of God and His purposes for man. This was of primary importance in the history of Israel. Moses gave his people the law, and the prophets taught them that God alone is God. That is why St. Paul could pose a rhetorical question to which he supplied the answer: "What advantage then hath the Jew?"; that is, what advantage does the Jew enjoy in comparison with the Gentile? He was quick to reply: "Much every way: chiefly, because that unto them were committed the oracles of God" (Rom. 3:1-2).

This meant little or nothing in the world of pagan culture. The best of the Gentiles, men such as Socrates·or Scipio, knew no more of truth than they could learn from the variable light of nature and reason. But the Jews were the appointed guardians of God's great self-revelation in the Scriptures, and the hinge on which their national history was to turn would be their conduct as its trustees.

The kingdom of Israel prospered under rulers who worshipped God, and honoured the law, and obeyed its precepts. It began to decline and plunged into headlong

ruin when it ignored God's word and will. The history of
Judaism for two thousand years bears witness to the reality
of this pattern. The Jews lost their identity as a nation while
they kept their identity as a people. It is only in this
generation that the world has seen their rehabilitation as a
national entity in the modern Israel. The centuries of
history that lie behind the people of Israel are all eloquent
in the evidence which they afford to God's great self-
revelation in the Old Testament. He made Himself known
to Adam and Abraham, to Moses and David, to Elijah and
Isaiah, and to all the prophets that the truth might reach
out to all generations.

The New Testament is the crowning glory of the Bible
because of its revelation of the Person of Christ. "God,
having of old time spoken unto the fathers in the prophets
... hath at the end of these days spoken unto us in His Son"
(Heb. 1:1-2, R.V.). Jesus Himself left no written record of
His Messianic message, but He set the seal of His own
unique authority on all that was written in the law and in
the prophets. He made it clear that this was the starting
point for all true understanding of His Messianic identity
and the purpose of His coming into the world (cf. Luke
24:27). A written record of His oral teaching was supplied
by the apostles and their companions, and they interpreted
its doctrine and ethic in their letters to the Churches.

No other first-century literature can compare with the
New Testament: it is so far superior to the literary relics of
that age in dignity of thought and the majesty of truth that
it carried its own *imprimatur* as God's final revelation to
man. The grand explanation of this lies in the fact that its
focus is always centred on Jesus, and that He is always seen
as both Lord and Christ. He came into the world to do one
thing; that was to die for the sin of the world: but such a
death would have had no value at all unless His own life
was absolutely free from the taint and guilt of sin. His life
was in fact marked by a moral perfection which men might
try to describe but could never invent; and His death was
invested with a sacrificial value which could only have been

derived from one who was sinless.

That perfection of character under every test and in every circumstance could not have been the mere literary product of a group of imperfect disciples. There was no one like Him: no saint or seer; no prophet or psalmist; He was unique. And the glory of the New Testament is that it shows how God sent His Son into this world that by means of Him our sins may be forgiven.

## 2. *Justification as an act of grace by faith alone*

The doctrine of Justification by faith alone is summed up in the classic statement of the Eleventh Article: "We are accounted righteous before God only for the merit of our Lord and Saviour Jesus Christ by faith, and not for our own works and deservings: wherefore that we are justified by faith only is a most wholesome doctrine and very full of comfort." We do not live in an age when men strive to accrue merit in the eyes of God by "their own works and deservings"; that is, by a round of religious observance which might vary from penance and fasting to pilgrimage and charities.

Nevertheless, perhaps unconsciously, many people today rely just as strongly on "their own works and deservings"; that is, on a good name, and a good life, and a good reputation. They make the same fundamental error as men did in medieval society; they fail to see that God who is just and holy can only account as righteous those who are truly righteous; and that is a claim which no man can make. Therefore the only ground on which we can hope to stand is that of a merit which is not our own: "the merit of our Lord and Saviour Jesus Christ"; and the only means by which we can take our stand on that ground is "by faith".

Let men ponder the words of Jacques Lefevre d' Etaples in 1512 before the voice of Martin Luther had been heard: "It is sheer profanity," he wrote, "to speak of the merit of works, especially in the presence of God. For plainly, merit does not ask a favour, but demands what is due; and to attribute merit to works is virtually to share the opinion of those who believe we can be justified by works, an error for which the Jews are most of all condemned. So let us be silent about the merit of our works, which amounts to very little, or rather nothing at all, and let us magnify the grace of God which is everything. He who defends merit respects man; but he who defends grace respects God."[1]

But how can God accept us as righteous when we know that we are sinful? And how can the merits of Christ become the ground for our acceptance instead of "our own works and deservings"? It is all in virtue of an exchange which is so great and so astonishing that our minds can scarcely take it in.

Jesus alone of all mankind measured up to God's standard of perfect obedience. Therefore He alone was qualified to stand as a substitute in the place where sinners deserve to stand. He who knew no sin was made to be sin for us that we who know no righteousness might be made the righteousness of God in Him. Our guilt was laid on His shoulders that His merits might be reckoned as ours.

Perhaps this has never been more clearly expressed outside the New Testament than in Martin Luther's letter to the troubled monk George Spenlein which he wrote in April 1516. "O my dear brother," so his counsel runs in a free English translation, "learn ... to despair of yourself and to say to Him, Thou Lord Jesus art my righteousness, and I am Thy sin; Thou hast taken what was mine, and hast given me what was Thine; Thou didst become what Thou was not so that what I was not I might become."[2]

But men may still ask, "How can these things be?" And the answer is as clear as a bell; it is, "By faith". Not that faith has any moral virtue; it is itself the gift of God. But faith will lead us to renounce all our own "works and deservings" and to rely on His merits alone. It was this great discovery which transformed Saul the Pharisee into Paul the Apostle, and no doctrine was more basic to his teaching on the forgiveness of sin, acceptance with God, present peace and lasting security. He had grasped this doctrine with a tenacity and an understanding which he never ceased to apply, and its strength and comfort ring out in his fearless challenge: "Who shall lay anything to the charge of God's elect? It is *God* that justifies" (Rom. 8:33).

### 3.  Forgiveness of sin on the sole ground of Christ's death

The redeeming love and atoning death of Christ are central in all Christian confessions of faith, although they may receive differing emphases on the part of theologians. It cannot be said too clearly that He was not compelled to die; that His death was in fact voluntary. He might have chosen to return into His Father's presence when He appeared with Moses and Elijah on the Mount of Glory; but He chose rather to speak of the death He would die in Jerusalem. He might have declined to return to Jerusalem where the Jews had sought to stone Him; but He chose rather to set His face like a flint as He went back even though He knew that at the end of the journey there stood a cross. He might have called on His Father and more than twelve legions of angels would have been at His command, but He chose rather to take up the cup of suffering and sacrifice and drain it all. Those who mocked Him seized on one thing. "He saved others," they said; "Himself He cannot save" (Matt. 27:42). That was true in a sense which they were too blind to perceive; He could not save Himself for the simple reason that He had come to save others.

Nor can it be said too strongly that He did not deserve to die; that His death was in fact sacrificial. His enemies might scrutinise His life with no other motive than to lay bare any detail, any word or action, on which they could frame an accusation. It was in vain; they could find no fault in Him at all. His conscience was stainless; His life was as clear as crystal. That was true in the day of His strength; He could face the most hostile crowd and throw out the challenge: "Which of you is able to convict Me of sin?" (John 8:46). No one spoke, because no one could. It was just as true in the hour of His weakness; He could look round the court room and repeat the challenge: "If I have spoken evil, bear witness of the evil" (John 18:23). No one did, because no one could. Pontius Pilate, Herod Antipas, and the dying thief all bore witness to the fact that there was nothing for which He deserved to die; sin had left no scar on Him from first to last.

Then why did he die? It was for the sake of others. That was the grand reason why He had come into the world; it was so that He might lay down His life as a ransom for ours. The most profound aspect of His death on the cross was "the travail of soul" (Isa, 53:11) that wrung from His heart the cry of desolation: "My God, My God, why hast Thou forsaken Me?" (Matt. 27:46). No one can tell what this must have involved; it is beyond us to follow Him into that region of soul darkness. But St. Paul was feeling after the truth when he declared that One who knew no sin had been *made sin* for us (2 Cor. 5:21), or *made a curse* for us (Gal. 3:13).

This pointed to something more than the fact that He was willing to take our sin and bear our curse; it meant that He identified Himself with it. He was sinless, but He was there to die for the sinful; and it was just because He knew no sin that He could be made sin for the sake of others.

If a fellow sinner should fall under sentence of death, it is conceivable that a friend might offer to take his place. But though I were that friend and were to die the death that he deserved, I could not clear his name from guilt. I, the innocent, would die, and the innocence would still be mine; he, the guilty, would live, and the guilt would still be his. Human law may allow for the transfer of penalty and punishment, but it cannot provide for an exchange of guilt.

This is the point where all human analogies break down; it brings us to the one great fact that makes the death of Christ unique. What the law cannot do because men are always sinful, God has now done through His Son who alone of all mankind had no sin of His own for which to die. God found a way for the transfer of guilt, and there has been a vast exchange. He sent His own dear Son to take our place, and pay our debt, and bear our guilt. He died the death that we deserve to die. He died as our Substitute and Sin-bearer. "Our hell He made His, that His heaven might be ours."[3] Never was there such love or mercy as this.

## 4.  *The necessity of the new birth by the Holy Spirit*

This is rooted in the famous words addressed to Nicodemus: "Verily, verily, I say unto thee, Except a man be born again, he cannot see the kingdom of God" (John 3:3). Seldom was the Lord Jesus so dogmatic in any utterance, but one comparable statement was addressed to the disciples: "Verily I say unto you, Except ye be converted," (except ye repent and believe), " ... ye shall not enter into the kingdom of heaven" (Matt. 18:3). He spoke of the new birth as something direct and personal. This fact has been hidden by the use of the pronoun *you* instead of *thee* in modern translations: "Marvel not that I said unto thee ...*thee* ... ye must be born again" (John 3:7).

This is something which has to do with each man or woman as one particular person; it is not the sort of experience which can be shared in a social spirit. To be born is a solitary event, and to die is a solitary event; it is one by one that we came into the world, and one by one that we go hence. The new birth is a need which we all have in common, but it is an experience which each must have for himself. That is why these words lay so much emphasis on the personal element: "Marvel not that I said unto *thee* ...*thee* ...*thee* ... ye must be born again."

They were not addressed to one of the vast crowds in Galilee, nor were they spoken to a sinner of scarlet hue or crimson dye. It was to one man that He spoke, and that man was not a prodigal ne'er-do-well, nor a money-grubbing taxation official, nor a social outcast, nor a dying bandit. It was Nicodemus, a religious man with a serious mind, a Pharisee and a ruler of the Jews, and he was dumbfounded at what he heard. How could a man be born when he is old? Could he enter this world a second time and have his life all over again? And the echo of those words in reply to his uncertainties still rings down the long and lonely corridors of time to fall on human ears and sound in human hearts as clear as ever. It is as though each of us were alone, just one soul in all the world, and we were to hear the voice of Jesus as did Nicodemus: "I say unto thee".

Seldom was the Lord Jesus so emphatic in any utterance; the same demand was made no less than three times in the space of five verses (John 3:3,5,7). He spoke of the new birth as something unique and essential. This is the one imperative necessity if we would see the Face of God. We might long for strength to race the lightning across the sky; but that would not be practical; much less would it be essential. But the new birth is so essential that no one can afford to neglect the warning which is inherent in the deliberate choice of one word: not *may,* but *must.*

It is little matter what else the new birth may involve; one thing is clear: this is the one experience which a man must have if he is to stand in the presence of God. It is not a case for human choice or option, something that man can please himself about. The King of that kingdom has made it plain: "You *must* be born again."

There are many things that men try to put in its place; but all to no avail. Education, for example, is an excellent thing, but it is not enough for God. Moral reform is not enough, nor self-discipline, nor church sacraments. A man may say his prayers, and read his Bible, and go to church on Sunday; but that is not enough. It is very hard to know how far a man may go in religious observance, and yet live and die without the grace of God in his soul. The new birth of which Nicodemus stood in need demands much more than a change of status; it means nothing less than a deep, inward, revolutionary change of nature. It means "a new heart ... and a new spirit" (Ezek. 36:26).

Nicodemus knew about that promise; what he was now

being told was that that promise *must* become a reality if he were to see the kingdom of God. That is the work of God's Holy Spirit in the inmost region of man's being, and that direct action by the Spirit of God in the soul of a man is as real as it is mysterious. No one doubts the reality of the wind because he can not see whence it comes or whither it goes; "so is every one that is born of the Spirit" (John 3:8). There is no more searching question a man can put to his own soul: "Have I been born again?" On the final answer to that question, that man's eternal destiny must turn.

## In Conclusion

Those four basic doctrines are the hallmarks of authentic Evangelical faith and teaching. Without them, the Evangelical movement in the Church of England would not survive.

It is true that Evangelicals have often exposed themselves to criticism for the defects which an all-too-dogmatic attitude can not fail to create. The masters of the Reformation were not immune from the perils of compromise and defection. The leaders of the spiritual awakening two hundred years ago were rent by the bitterness and invective of angry controversy. The exponents and adherents of the Evangelical school of thought in our own day are often guilty of a certain smugness or self-conceit in their general attitude. But when one has allowed for all the weakness or failure of the past or present, this school of faith and thought has shown remarkable resilience. It still persists with a vitality which shows no sign of an early decline.

This means one thing. The secret of Evangelical continuity in the Church lies in the doctrines of grace which have gripped so many people from generation to generation, and not in the people who have been gripped by them.

Then what manner of men ought we to be if we would be known as Evangelicals? No Evangelical can live as though he were just a private individual; he cannot go into retreat from those with whom he disagrees. We are in the Church and of the Church, and we must relate to the society in which we find ourselves. Double care is therefore necessary not to allow worldly practice to rub off on our lives. We must maintain high spiritual standards and moral values. And we need to remind ourselves that there will always be a line beyond which we must not permit ourselves to go. That line may be invisible; there is no rule of thumb to say just where it runs. We need grace and humility, openness and discernment, if we are so to live that we will commend as well as uphold all that the word "Evangelical" ought to mean.

# NOTES

## Preface

1 E. L. Woodward, *The Age of Reform, 1815–1870*, p.485.
2 Ibid.
3 R.K. Ensor, *England, 1870–1914*, p.138.
4 Ibid, p.140, footnote 1.
5 cf. H.W.K. Mowll, *Seeing All The World*, pp.92–3.

## Chapter 1

1 Peter Toon and Michael Smout, *John Charles Ryle, Evangelical Bishop*, p. 7.
2 Peter Toon, *J.C. Ryle, A Self-Portrait*, p.4.
3 *Self-Portrait*, p.36.
4 Ibid., p.37.
5 Ibid., p.8.
6 Ibid., p.11.
7 Ibid., p.10.
8 Ibid., p.12.
9 Ibid., p.12.
10 Ibid., p.13.
11 Ibid., p.15.
12 Ibid., p.22.
13 Ibid.
14 Ibid., p.17.

[15] cf. Toon and Smout, p.15.
[16] *Self-Portrait,* p.20.
[17] cf. Maurice H. Fitzgerald, *A Memoir of Herbert Edward Ryle,* p.28.
[18] *Self-Portrait*, p.20.
[19] cf. Fitzgerald, p.2; cf. *Self-Portrait,* p.21.
[20] *Self-Portrait,* p.19.
[21] *Knots Untied*, p.102.
[22] *Self-Portrait,* pp.20–1.
[23] Ibid, p.30.
[24] Toon and Smout, p.21.
[25] cf. Fitzgerald, p.3.
[26] *Self-Portrait,* p.47.
[27] cf. Fitzgerald, p.36.
[28] Ibid., p.64.
[29] Ibid., p.133.
[30] *Self-Portrait*, p.21.
[31] Ibid., p.29.
[32] cf. David Newsome, *The Parting of Friends,* p.64.
[33] E.L. Woodward, *The Age of Reform, 1815–1870,* p.470.
[34] Ibid., p.471.
[35] cf. Toon and Smout, p.19.
[36] cf. J.S. Reynolds, 'Towards A Full Treatment' *(The English Churchman,* June 3rd, 1977).
[37] *Self-Portrait,* p.29.
[38] Ibid.
[39] Ibid., p.30.
[40] cf. Fitzgerald, p.2; *Self-Portrait, p.33.*
[41] cf. J.S. Reynolds, 'Towards A Full Treatment' *(The English Churchman,* June 3rd, 1977).
[42] *Self-Portrait,* p.36.
[43] cf. *Knots Untied,* p.102.
[44] *Self-Portrait, p.35.*
[45] Ibid., pp.39–40.
[46] *The Record,* June 15th, 1900; cf. Toon and Smout, p.26, *Self-Portrait,* p.39.
[47] *Self-Portrait,* p.40.
[48] Ibid., p.40.

[49] cf. *The Record,* June 15th, 1900, cited by Toon and Smout, p. 109, but not available to me.

[50] cf. W.H.Griffith Thomas, *The Work of the Ministry,* p.185.

[51] J.W. Diggle, *Quiet Hours with the Ordinal,* p.72.

[52] *Self-Portrait,* p.35.

[53] Ibid., p.40.

[54] Ibid., pp.41-2.

[55] Ibid.

[56] Ibid., p.43.

*Chapter 2*

[1] *Self-Portrait,* p.47.

[2] L.E. O'Rorke, *The Life and Friendships of Catherine Marsh,* p.41.

[3] *Self-Portrait,* pp.45-6.

[4] cf. G.W. Hart, *Bishop J.C. Ryle, Man of Granite,* p.4.

[5] *Self-Portrait,* p.49.

[6] *Self-Portrait,* p.52.

[7] Ibid., p.51.

[8] *The Record,* June 15th, 1900; cited by Toon and Smout, p.31.

[9] *Self-Portrait,* p.53.

[10] Ibid.

[11] Ibid., p.56.

[12] W.F. Machray, *The Right Reverend John Charles Ryle,* p.7.

[13] *Self-Portrait,* p.59.

[14] L.E. O'Rorke, ibid., p.41.

[15] cf. M. Guthrie Clarke, *John Charles Ryle,* p.12.

[16] *Self-Portrait, p.63.*

[17] *The Upper Room, p.54.*

[18] *Self-Portrait,* p.62.

[19] Ibid., p.63.

[20] Ibid., p.67.
[21] Toon and Smout, p.97; *Self-Portrait,* p.74.
[22] *Self-Portrait,* p.69.
[23] cf. *Self-Portrait,* p.68.
[24] See Toon and Smout, p.41.
[25] See E.D.H. Tollemache, *The Tollemaches of Helmingham and Ham,* pp.167–70.
[26] *Self-Portrait,* p.43.
[27] Ibid., p.71.
[28] Ibid., p.75.
[29] Toon and Smout, p.41.
[30] Ibid., p.45.
[31] *Self-Portrait,* p.72.
[32] Ibid., p.71.
[33] cf. Toon and Smout, p.49.
[34] *Self-Portrait,* p.62.
[35] Crockford's *Clerical Directory,* 1882.
[36] W.F. Machray, ibid., p.44.
[37] G.R. Balleine; *A History of The Evangelical Party,* p.215.
[38] G.H.G. Hewitt, *Let the People Read,* p.42.
[39] Frederic Barker, Manuscript diary, 1855.
[40] Mrs. Barker, Manuscript Diary and Letters.
[41] W.F. Machray: Ibid., p.44.
[42] G.R. Balleine, Ibid., p.220, footnote.
[43] *Self-Portrait,* p.73.
[44] Ibid.
[45] Toon and Smout, p.42; but see *Self-Portrait,* p.75.
[46] *Self-Portrait,* p.76.
[47] See *Self-Portrait,* pp.79–81.
[48] *Self-Portrait,* p.81.
[49] *Christian Leaders in the Last Century,* p.280.
[50] *Self-Portrait,* p.81.
[51] cf. *The Tollemaches of Helmingham and Ham,* p.167.
[52] Ibid., p.170.
[53] Ibid., p.171.
[54] cf. Toon and Smout, p.50.
[55] *Self-Portrait,* p.80.

*Chapter 3*

1  *Memoir of H.E. Ryle*, p.14.
2  *Principles for Churchmen*, p.398.
3  *Memoir of H.E. Ryle*, p.13.
4  Ibid., p.11.
5  Ibid., p.36.
6  Ibid., p.37.
7  Ibid., p.134.
8  See *Self-Portrait*, pp.VI–VII.
9  See *Memoir of H.E. Ryle*, pp.1–9.
10  *Ibid., p.13.*
11  *Quoted by Toon and Smout, pp.51–2.*
12  *Memoir of H.E. Ryle*, p.11.
13  Ibid., p.13.
14  Toon and Smout, p.55.
15  *Self-Portrait*, Part Two, p.87.
16  Toon and Smout, p.55.
17  Quoted in Toon and Smout, p.56.
18  Toon and Smout, p.56.
19  H.C.G. Moule, *The Evangelical School in the Church of England*, p.58.
20  W. Knight, *Memoir of Henry Venn*, p.312.
21  H. Gresford Jones, *F.J. Chavasse*, p.29.
22  *Holiness*, p.121.
23  *Old Paths*, p.187.
24  *Light From Old Times*, p.viii.
25  *Christian Leaders of the Last Century*, p.iv.
26  *Light From Old Times*, p.181.
27  *What Do We Owe to the Reformation: and Why Were the Reformers Burnt?*
28  *Light From Old Times*, p.54.
29  *Knots Untied*, p.24.
30  W.F. Machray, ibid., p.16.
31  E.L. Woodward, *The Age of Reform, 1815–1870*, pp. 485–6.
32  F. Warre Cornish, *The English Church in the Nineteenth Century*, Vol. 2, p.218.

33 *Old Paths,* p.34.
34 *Expository Thoughts on St. John's Gospel,* Vol. 1, p.vii.
35 *The Upper Room,* pp.164; 172.
36 Eugene Stock, *The History of the Church Missionary Society,* Vol. 2, p.342.
37 Ibid, Vol. 2, p.455.
38 *Principles for Churchmen,* pp.97–8.
39 *What is Written About the Lord's Supper?,* p.30.
40 cf. Toon and Smout, p.59.
41 *Principles For Churchmen,* p.62.
42 G.R. Balleine, ibid., p.215.
43 *Principles For Churchmen,* pp.78–9.
44 Ibid., p.78.
45 *Expository Thoughts on St. Matthew's Gospel,* p.v.
46 J.C. MacDonnell, *The Life of Archbishop Magee,* Vol. 1, p.119
47 Ibid, Vol. 1, p.195.
48 Eugene Stock, *My Recollections,* pp.90–1.
49 W.F. Machray, ibid., p.13.
50 Ibid.
51 *Knots Untied,* p.2.
52 Ibid., p.30.

Chapter 4

1 cf. Toon and Smout, p.51.
2 Ibid., p.112, footnote 42.
3 Ibid., p.51.
4 cf. Toon and Smout, p.56.
5 Ibid., p.65.
6 *Principles for Churchmen,* p.60.
7 Ibid., p.xii.
8 Quoted by M. Guthrie Clark, ibid., p.30.
9 Eugene Stock, *History of the Church Missionary Society,* Vol. 3, p.8.

10  *Knots Untied,* p.190.
11  *Charges and Addresses,* p.154.
12  *Memoir of H.E. Ryle,* p.31.
13  cf. G.R. Balleine, ibid., p.238.
14  cf. J.C. Pollock, *The Keswick Story,* p.33.
15  John Kent, *Holding The Fort, Studies in Victorian Revivalism,* p.312.
16  *Holiness,* p.1.
17  Ibid., p.xvii.
18  John Kent, ibid., p.314.
19  *Holiness,* p.xxix.
20  Ibid., p.viii.
21  *Simplicity in Preaching* (reprinted as Chapter Three in *The Upper Room*).
22  *The Upper Room,* p.36.
23  Ibid., pp. 52–3.
24  cf. W.F. Machray; ibid., p.45.
25  *Principles For Churchmen,* p.164.
26  *Memoir of H.E. Ryle,* p.14.
27  *Holiness,* pp.388–9 cf. *Old Paths,* pp. 415–6.
28  *Expository Thoughts on the Gospel of St. Matthew,* p.iv.
29  *Expository Thoughts on the Gospel of St. John,* Vol. 1, p.xii.
30  *Knots Untied,* p.iv.
31  Ibid., p.1.
32  *Practical Religion,* p.v.
33  *Old Paths,* pp.vii–viii.
34  *Practical Religion,* p.vi.
35  *The Churchman,* January 1880.
36  A.R.M. Finlayson; *The Life of Canon Fleming,* p.178, footnote.
37  cf. Toon and Smout, p.58.

*Chapter 5*

1  Toon and Smout, p.74.

[2] William Macquarie Cowper, *The Episcopate of the Right Rev. Frederic Barker,* p.23.
[3] Arthur R. M. Finlayson, *Life of Canon Fleming,* pp.179–180.
[4] G.E. Buckle, *Letters of Queen Victoria,* Second Series, Vol.III, p.78.
[5] cf. W.F. Machray, ibid., pp.13 ff.; A.R.M. Finlayson, ibid., pp.178–9, footnote.
[6] cf. G.R. Balleine, ibid., p.221.
[7] Toon and Smout, p.74.
[8] Richard Hobson, *What Hath God Wrought,* p.139.
[9] *The Record,* May 7th, 1880, cf. Toon and Smout, p.73.
[10] *The Record,* June 15th, 1880; cf. Toon and Smout, p.73.
[11] J.G. Lockhart; *Charles Lindley, Viscount Halifax,* (1935), Vol.I, p.249.
[12] *The Church Times,* July 2nd, 1880.
[13] cf. G.R. Balleine, ibid., p.221; Toon and Smout, p.77.
[14] *Charges and Addresses,* p.69.
[15] Ibid., p.4; cf. p.145; p.342.
[16] Ibid., p.69.
[17] Ibid., p.69.
[18] W.F. Machray, p.23.
[19] *Charges and Addresses,* p.36.
[20] W.F. Machray, p.23.
[21] *Charges and Addresses,* p.62.
[22] Ibid., pp.67–8; cf. p.342.
[23] *Charges and Addresses,* p.70.
[24] Ibid., p.68.
[25] Ibid., p.342.
[26] Toon and Smout, p.76.
[27] *Charges and Addresses,* p.14.
[28] Ibid., pp.79–80.
[29] Ibid., p.187.
[30] Ibid., p.289.
[31] Ibid., p.146.
[32] cf. Toon and Smout, p.76.
[33] W.F. Machray, p.17.
[34] M. Guthrie Clark, p.22.

35 Albert Mitchell, *The Record,* July 11th 1941.
36 Mary Church, *The Life and Letters of Dean Church,* p.336.
37 *Charges and Addresses,* p.17.
38 Ibid., p.28.
39 W.F. Machray, ibid., p.25.
40 cf. Toon and Smout, p.87.
41 Richard Hobson, ibid., p.170.
42 W.F. Machray, ibid., pp.25–6.
43 W.F. Machray: ibid., p.27.
44 Ibid.
45 A.C. Benson, *Edward White Benson,* Vol. 2, p.243.
46 *Charges and Addresses,* p.133.
47 Ibid., p.135.
48 W.F. Machray, ibid., p.30.
49 *Charges and Addresses,* pp.247–8.
50 cf. *Knots Untied* (1896 edition), p.iii.
51 *Principles For Churchmen,* p.xxvii.
52 *The Upper Room,* p.vii.

*Chapter 6*

1 *Memoir of H.E. Ryle,* p.10.
2 Ibid., p.358.
3 Ibid.
4 Ibid., p.302.
5 Ibid., p.303.
6 Ibid., p.358.
7 *Memoir of H.E. Ryle,* p.36.
8 Ibid. p.131.
9 G.L. Prestige, *The Life of Charles Gore,* p.85.
10 *Memoir of H.E. Ryle,* p.134.
11 Ibid., p.350.
12 *Charges and Addresses,* p.339.
13 Ibid., p.188.

14 Ibid., p.339.
15 Toon and Smout, p.118, footnote 46.
16 *Charges and Addresses,* p.342.
17 Richard Hobson; ibid., pp.193, 279.
18 cf. Toon and Smout, p.82.
19 Richard Hobson, ibid., p.317; cf. *Memoir of H.E. Ryle,* p.53.
20 Richard Hobson, ibid., p.166.
21 Eugene Stock, *History of The Church Missionary Society,* Vol. 3, 281, footnote.
22 H.C.G. Moule, *The Evangelical School in The Church of England,* p.112.
23 *The Record,* August 12th 1892; cf. Eugene Stock, Vol. 3, p.282.
24 *Charges and Addresses,* p.110.
25 cf. Eugene Stock; ibid., Vol. 3, p.282.
26 W.F. Machray, ibid., p.32.
27 Ibid., pp.36–7.
28 *The Protestant Observer* (date unknown).
29 *Memoir of H.E. Ryle,* p.364.
30 J.C. Pollock, ibid., p.33.
31 *Memoir of H.E. Ryle,* p.134.
32 Richard Hobson, ibid., p.294.
33 Ibid., p.294.
34 Toon and Smout, p.90.
35 *Memoir of H.E. Ryle,* p.133.
36 *Charges and Addresses,* p.341; cf. p.325.
37 Richard Hobson, ibid., p.169.
38 cf. John Kent; ibid., p.353.
39 cf. Toon and Smout, p.84.
40 J.C. Pollock, ibid., pp.77–8.
41 *Charges and Addresses,* p.291.
42 J.C. Pollock, *A Cambridge Movement,* p.132.
43 Hobson, ibid., pp.180–1.
44 J.C. Pollock, *Moody Without Sankey,* p.270.
45 cf. M.L. Loane, *Hewn From the Rock,* pp. 124–6.
46 Eugene Stock, Vol. IV, pp.397–8; cf. Toon and Smout, p.93.

[47] cf. Toon and Smout, p.92.
[48] *What Is Written About The Lord's Supper?* p.1.
[49] *Charges and Addresses* (1978 edition), pp xii–xiii.
[50] E.L. Woodward, *The Age of Reform 1815–1870*, p.486.
[51] Georgina Battiscombe, *Shaftesbury 1801–1885*, p.103.
[52] G.W. Hart, ibid., p.21.
[53] *Memoir of H.E. Ryle*, p.36.
[54] *The Record*, July 11th, 1941.
[55] L.E. O'Rorke, *The Life and Friendships of Catherine Marsh*, p.324.
[56] *Memoir of H.E. Ryle*, p.133.
[57] Richard Hobson, ibid., p.273.
[58] Ibid., p.279.
[59] Eugene Stock, Vol.4, pp.8; 428.
[60] *Memoir of H.E. Ryle*, p.133.
[61] Richard Hobson, ibid., pp.286–7.
[62] Ibid., p.289.
[63] *Charges and Addresses*, p.367.
[64] Ibid., p.368.
[65] *Memoir of H.E. Ryle*, p.134.
[66] Ibid., pp.170–1.
[67] Ibid., p.135.
[68] Richard Hobson, ibid., pp. 327–8.
[69] J.B. Lancelot, *F.J. Chavasse*, p.143.

## Appendix

[1] Quoted by Philip Edgecumbe Hughes, *A Commentary on the Epistle to the Hebrews*, p.461.
[2] Martin Luther, *Works*, Vol. 1, p.33.
[3] Philip Edgecumbe Hughes, ibid., p.120.

# INDEX